STEPPING INTO THE LIGHT

REFLECTIONS OF A HOSPICE NURSE

Kaye Brinkman Howell

STEPPING INTO THE LIGHT
Copyright 2024
Kaye Brinkman Howell

All rights reserved.

ISBN: 979-8-89480-091-2

The stories related in this book are true. Names and certain details have been changed to protect the privacy of the people involved.

Cover Design by Raney Day Creative, LLC
Cover images generated with Midjourney AI

All songs are public domain with the exception of *God on the Mountain* and *Each One, Reach One*, which are used with permission.

Brinkman Howell Publishing

DEDICATION

To my husband Chuck. I remember how raw my emotions were because many of these stories were happening as I was writing them. I remember how loving and patient you were when I came home crying on so many of those difficult days. You have always been my strength! And thank you for all the hours you spent editing this manuscript. I could not have done this without you. I love you, baby.

To my parents, Earl and Catherine Brinkman, for showing me the way to Jesus and for being my pattern for living. What a privilege it was to be at your bedsides when you each took one last breath on earth and your next breath in Jesus' arms. It was a time of great sadness yet rejoicing in knowing that you had made it safely Home! I miss you both every day. What a comfort in knowing that we will be spending eternity together!

Earl Ray Brinkman
April 28, 1924 - December 15, 2008

Catherine Buttram Brinkman
September 19, 1923 - February 7, 2015

Most of all, thank You Jesus
for Your amazing grace!
You have changed my life forever!

CONTENTS

Dedication	iii
Foreword	v
Acknowledgments	viii
Chapter 1 — Mary's Song	1
Chapter 2 — Mark's Witness	15
Chapter 3 — Please Hear Me, Shane	25
Chapter 4 — Miss Emily's Secret	35
Chapter 5 — Bobby's Promise	43
Chapter 6 — Granny Mama's Birthday	51
Chapter 7 — Don't Let Me Die Like My Father	57
Chapter 8 — Angels on the Balcony	67
Chapter 9 — When Jenny Sang	73
Chapter 10 — A Second Chance	87
Chapter 11 — Home for Christmas	95
Chapter 12 — The Confession	103
Chapter 13 — Six Weeks to Live	111
Chapter 14 — A Praying Woman	119
Index of Songs	125
The Sinner's Prayer	126
About the Author	127

FOREWORD

Many people are not aware of the choices available to them and their loved ones until they are faced with a life-limiting illness. The concept of hospice and palliative care began in England in the 1950's and became an alternative for people who did not want to spend their last days in a hospital setting.

Palliative care is available for many life-threatening conditions, including cancer. It enables patients to continue to receive treatments that may *cure* their illness, and helps with pain and symptom control. Strong emphasis is placed on helping the caregiver to receive support and education to deal with a serious illness.

Hospice care is a type of palliative care regulated by Medicare. It is typically for patients who have six months or less to live. It becomes appropriate when the focus of treatment becomes *comfort* instead of curative. It also has a strong emphasis on emotional support for the families involved. But Hospice services do not automatically end at six months. If the patient's doctor certifies that the patient is terminally ill, the hospice benefit continues.

While many patients are able to receive care in their home, nursing home, or assisted living residence, there are those who choose to spend their last days in a hospice inpatient facility where around-the-clock care and support are offered.

The hospice philosophy of care is a team approach. The team includes family members, a physician, nurse, home health aide, social worker (counselor), volunteer, and chaplain. The goal is to provide skilled nursing care, spiritual care, pain control, and symptom management. Strong emphasis is on the family during the grieving process, and bereavement services can last up to 12 months after the patient passes away.

Patients do not have to wait until their last few days of life to receive services. A much better outcome happens when services are provided while the patient can still make his or her own decisions.

I found that Christians of strong faith often felt that they were giving up or that they were not keeping their faith convictions if they become a hospice patient. That was not true. I told my patients that we would pray every day for the Lord to intervene with His healing touch. I also assured them that in the meantime we would keep them as comfortable as possible.

Hospice nursing is a calling. I wanted to keep my patients strong in their faith. Hospice can be a special, blessed event in which the family and their loved one can be comforted, even in the midst of their grief.

Looking back, I believe that my hospice experience was unusual because I became so emotionally involved. Many of those families are still my friends today. Several of us had churches in common and I found it difficult to separate my personal life from my nursing responsibilities. I often took home cooked meals to them. I had dinner gatherings in my home attended by patient families who had become friends, and we were able to share and understand issues that were common to survivors. Most patients had my phone number. And they knew that they had my prayers.

I thank God for that season in my life. Although not typical hospice care, it surely met their needs, and was the most fulfilling time that I have ever experienced.

To God be the Glory.

ACKNOWLEDGMENTS

My thanks:

To Carolyn Meiller (Reba Rhyne-author) for your encouragement and patience in keeping me on track with this manuscript. As a published author many times over, your guidance has been a wealth of information. Thank you for believing in me. I treasure our friendship.

To Shirley Lips and others who read the manuscript and made productive comments and corrections.

To Dawn Staymates for her formatting genius.

To Ken Raney for the beautiful cover.

To Sheriff Grady Judd and his deputies who insisted that they be nearby when I went to pronounce a patient in the middle of the night. Thank you for making me feel safe.

And to all of those whose lives have intersected with mine. You know who you are, and you know how much I love you.

STEPPING INTO THE LIGHT

REFLECTIONS OF A HOSPICE NURSE

Kaye Brinkman Howell

Chapter One

Mary's Song

When I pulled into her driveway, I could hear her crying. Ovarian cancer with metastasis to the bone had finally conquered her body at only 45 years of age. I could not fathom what she had been through for the previous five years. Her husband and mother were there, and we sat at her kitchen table to complete the paperwork that had to be done.

I had never seen anyone cry as much as she did that day. Tears were pouring down her cheeks, and tissues were damp all over the table. About every third sentence she would say, *"Lord, You know I'm ready. Just take me right now. You know I can't stand this pain anymore."*

I was trying to get her medical history and found that she had never really had pain control. The last few months had been the worst, and she was now at the point of hysteria. When I asked her what her pain level was, if *zero* was no pain and *ten* was the worst she could imagine, she cried *fifteen*.

The countertop was covered with pill bottles, some empty, some full. No one in the house could tell me what medications were for what symptoms, and what, if any, medications she had taken that day. Everything was in a state of confusion.

I called her doctor for medication orders, and when we had signed the necessary paperwork, her husband helped her back into the bedroom. She cried with each slow step. I followed her into the bedroom and gave her medication for agitation and a strong dose of narcotics for her pain. I put my arms around her, prayed aloud, cried, and massaged her gently until she could relax and the medication could become effective. It took three hours. We were both crying, praying, and quoting scripture. It was one of the most painful memories I have of her suffering.

I was angry that her previous caregivers had discharged her because she had not died within their *six-month* limit. I was angry because there were no teaching materials in the home. I was angry because there was no medication box to sort out the dozens of pills that she was taking at various times throughout the day and night.

I was angry that the family had not been taught what medications were for what symptoms. I was angry that someone so young and sweet had to be suffering so terribly. And I was deeply touched that through all of this, she was not blaming God. Instead, she just cried and begged to go home to heaven, constantly expressing her love for the Savior and thanking Him for being with her.

Making sure that all her medications were properly labeled, I ordered the new ones she needed plus a large medication box. A hospital bed, so she could get up and down more easily, was next on my list.

When her pain decreased to a level *four*, she asked if she could go into the living room to be with her family. Someone had brought over some bean soup and cornbread, and when I left, she was eating, curled up on the recliner.

Although I felt an instant connection with her, I never dreamed what an impact she would have on my life. I crossed all the emotional boundaries with Mary. I just couldn't help it. She was so easy to love. I got to know her visitors and family and the impact that she had made on their lives. I always looked forward to the nursing visits that we would have. With the exception of a single weekend when I was out of town, I saw her every day for the remaining six weeks of her life.

Mary was a Christian and had a deep and intimate relationship with Jesus Christ. She had been very active in her small church, serving as the organist. The highlights of her week were being in both services on Sundays and then Wednesday night prayer meetings. Much of the time she had to be helped into the building and often had to leave early. But she told me that she wanted to go for as long as she possibly could because that gave her joy and strength to face the next day.

Realizing how difficult it was for her to attend her church made me feel guilty for the excuses I often used for not attending mine.

The next day I filled her pillbox for the week, organized all her medications, and made sure that there were written instructions. We got her settled in her new hospital bed but encouraged her to be up as much as she felt like it. That day she greeted me with a tolerable pain level of *three*.

Her symptoms seemed to be in a three-day cycle. On the first day, she would be in severe pain. The next, she would be zonked with meds, and on the third day she would be feeling more energetic, without pain, and anxious to go to church. Then the cycle would begin all over again.

Although the severity of her symptoms decreased as time went on, the cycle continued. We battled depression that followed her lack of control over the circumstances, and we adjusted her medications every day.

～

During one of our heart-to-heart talks, she told me that she didn't understand why she was afraid to die. She said she knew she was saved, was anxious to see Jesus, and that she was ready to go to heaven, but that this feeling of fear surrounded her.

I told her that she was probably afraid of the *dying process*. "You have never died," I said. "*You don't know what it will be like, if you will have pain, or if you will panic at the last minute.*" She nodded in agreement and said that made sense to her.

I felt the Lord directing me to tell her that there would be no struggle, no pain, and no fear. I said that she would take one last breath here and the next breath in Jesus' arms. I told her that it would be such a sweet and easy transition, that her family would be amazed. We prayed together before I left, and she seemed relieved.

～

When I arrived the next day, she met me at the door. *"Get in here. You need to hear what happened to me last night,"* she said.

She began telling me that when she went to bed, she wasn't sure whether she was asleep or awake, but that Jesus had called her by name. He had said, *"Mary, when I am ready for you, it will happen just as your nurse described. You will take one last breath here, and the next breath will be in my arms. You will not be afraid."*

She was at peace with her impending death from that day on. Every time I tell her story, the same feeling overwhelms me, just as it did the day that she shared it with me. I'll never forget that.

~

Mary had so many friends. Most of them were from her church, and they were there often. Whether she was having a good day or a bad one, she was always uplifting them. She seemed to be their strength. When they came to bring her flowers, cards, and meals, they would leave with her words of faith and encouragement. Many times, I would hear, *"I came here to pray for Sister Mary and to encourage her, but here she is with all her pain and suffering, and she ministered to me!"*

She was loved by so many people, from the elderly lady who was too weak to climb the steps into Mary's house and had to have her son carry her inside, to the teenagers who were always around. She had a wonderful way of making each one feel special and blessed.

~

I remember one day when she was especially weak. I was talking to her about just letting go. She said that her son was not where he needed to be spiritually, and that she was having a hard time letting go for fear that she would never see him again.

We talked about how her prayers and the prayers of so many others, could continue to work in his life, and that long after she was gone, he could find God's saving grace. She lay back in the recliner and thought about that for a long time.

∼

The bond that Mary and I developed was strong. I found myself thinking about her and praying for her throughout the day. Our common ground was Jesus.

We had meaningful times sharing scripture, praying together, singing, and praising God for His goodness. I looked forward to every visit. It gave me time to look inward and see just how deep my commitment to the Lordship of Christ really was.

She taught me that the God in the good times is still the God in the bad times. She was always praising Him. And each day became a spiritual renewal for me. I felt as though I had known her forever. We shared a friendship and love that was very special. In many ways, it was a wonderful time.

∼

Mary had a sweet and loving family. Her husband was attentive to her needs. Often, he and I would talk about what he would do after she was gone. I told him that he needed to let her know that it was all right for her to die. People often need permission to die. They need the assurance that the people they are leaving behind will be all right. He cried for her, and he cried for his own loss.

Mary's mother was very ill with heart and lung problems, and always pulled her oxygen tank behind her when she came to visit. We talked about how hard it is for parents to bury their children. Mama Jean often was so weak and sick that I wondered which one of them would die first. Mama Jean had let Mary go long before I knew them. She had seen Mary in pain for so many years that she had prayed that the Lord would end her suffering. Of all the family, she was probably the one most ready to release her precious daughter.

∼

Mary had a grown son. Although he lived close by, I did not get to know him until that last week. He told me later that his mother had been through so many bad times and bounced back, that he thought she would do it again this time.

When I realized that we were talking about *days* and not *weeks*, I called him and asked if he would meet with me. I told him that she would not recover this time unless the Lord intervened. I also told him what she had said about his relationship with God.

Although it was a painful time for both of us, I told him that he needed to do whatever it took to make peace with his mother so that she could let go. I don't know what was said between them, but things were different after that night. There was an acute awareness of her impending death, and he came with his family and stayed.

∼

The weekend before Mary died, I took a much-needed break and let the on-call nurse see her. When I received the report on Monday morning that Mary had requested a catheter because it was just too hard for her to get out of bed and go to the bathroom, I knew that she had finally given up. That was the one thing that she had fought against for so long.

I felt a strange sadness.

Diapers came next, and she had a long day of diarrhea. I was cleaning her up for the umpteenth time when she started crying. She said that she didn't want to be a bother to anyone, and that she was so sorry that she had no control.

"Why is this happening? I feel so bad about this," she cried. I told her that she was getting ready for heaven and that she did not want to go flying through the pearly gates yelling for the ladies' room. We both collapsed in laughter! It helped to ease the tension that she was feeling as her condition continued to deteriorate.

∼

Mary had personally taken care of her final arrangements months before. She had gone to the funeral home, chosen her casket, and picked out her burial plot. She wanted her favorite songs sung at her funeral. She had asked me several times if I would sing, but I told her that there was no way that I could. I knew that I would not be emotionally ready. So, we sang her songs together, Mary in her hospital bed and me beside her. We sang our hearts out. And we cried because we knew that was all we would ever have. She told me that she loved me every time I saw her. She said I was her best friend. I tried to explain to her what an impact she was having on my life.

Mary asked us to hang the beautiful pink lace dress that she had chosen to wear on her bedroom door. She just wanted to look at it. Maybe she thought that it would hasten the end. Many times, during those last days, she would get frustrated with us because we would not go ahead and let her wear it.

She was so ready to go.

We were administering pain medication every four hours around the clock. She was on high doses of narcotics to keep her comfortable. Ovarian cancer is typically one of the most difficult to manage in terms of pain control and we fought it all the way. But I had promised her that I would not let pain overtake her in the end, and thankfully, she was pain-free.

She talked about her daddy and other relatives and friends who had gone on before. She said they were standing in her room, waiting for her to join them. *I believe that she saw them.*

The day before she died, Mary was very agitated. She thrashed about in her bed, trying to get up. She talked about things that made no sense to us. She had not eaten in several days, and her urine output dwindled to almost nothing as her kidneys shut down. She cried a lot. Church friends came and went.

When I arrived at her home the next morning, they told me that she had slipped into a coma during the night. She was propped up in bed, looking very small under the covers. Her mouth was open, and her breathing was irregular. I could not get her blood pressure. Her feet and hands were blue. She had a fever. Her breathing became more and more labored.

∼

About an hour later, she began having periods of apnea (not breathing). She would take a shallow breath and then stop breathing. It happened many times.

I called her husband in from the carport. *"It's time,"* I told him. We surrounded her bed. Just as God had promised, she took that last breath and slipped into the waiting arms of the Savior she loved so dearly.

For a moment, we all just stood there. I joined hands with those around her bed and her pastor prayed, *"Thank You, Lord, for giving her to us to love, and thank You for her beautiful life that has impacted all of us. We thank You for taking her now because she is in Your presence. All her pain is gone."*

I looked around the room fully expecting to see her spirit form being raised, but there was nothing but a quiet, peaceful presence in the room. Her face was radiant.

∼

They asked for some time before the funeral home was called. It was a time of rejoicing, even amid great sadness. A steady stream of visitors came through her home, folks who had loved her so much.

Her friend and I put on the nightgown that she had requested and propped her up on pillows. She looked like she was sleeping.

Mary's passing was especially hard on her son. He cried and agonized over his loss. I cried and agonized for mine. I felt as though I had lost a family member. This was My Mary. My special patient. My sweet friend.

We had taken such good care of her and we felt so relieved that she wasn't suffering anymore. But I was grieving because I would never hear her little childlike voice again, and because I would never be able to hug her and feel her love. *Although she was not aware of it, she had become my strength through her darkest hours.* I knew that I would always think about her and that my life would be changed because I had known her.

∽

I remember being surprised at how nice she looked at the funeral home visitation. I had never seen her blonde hair all done up. The lines in her face, etched so deeply with pain, had smoothed out. She had suffered so much, but God, as He promised, had wiped away her tears.

She lay there, the picture of peace. My Mary, who had always looked like a little girl with her hair straight and her little mouth sunken in, looked like a grown woman. She was beautiful.

I gave the eulogy at her funeral. She had touched me in a way that no one else ever had, and I wanted to talk about it. I wanted people to know what she had done in six short weeks. I wanted them to know that I loved her, too.

∽

When I sang at her little church a few months later, it was like a family reunion. The people that I had come to know during her final days were still smiling and praising God for the impact she had made on their lives. What a wonderful legacy she left.

I often tell her story when I'm singing, and people everywhere have been touched by her courageous dying.

When I recorded my first CD project, I dedicated it to her memory. Her family was so pleased. It seemed like the perfect thing to do.

∽

I will never forget her! I was privileged to be her nurse, her prayer partner, and her friend. She reminded me that the God in the good times is still the God in the bad times.

She kept the faith, and she died with dignity. She showed me how a Christian can be victorious through the shadows of death as she courageously stepped into the light.

I still think about you every day, Mary, and I will always love you. Thank you for the lessons in courage that I learned from you. You made such an incredible difference in my life.

God on the Mountain

Life is easy when you're up on the mountain.
And you've got peace of mind
like you've never known.
But things change when you're down in the valley.
Don't lose faith, for you're never alone.

∽

You talk of faith when you're up on the mountain.
Talk comes so easy when life's at its best.
Now it's down in the valley of trials and temptation,
That's when your faith is really put to the test.

∽

For the God on the mountain is still God in the valley.
When things go wrong, He'll make them right.
And the God of the good times
is still God of the bad times.
The God of the day is still God in the night.

Tracy G. Dartt

Chapter 2

Mark's Witness

Mark's story really began eight years before his death. A small family living in an isolated area in rural Florida had a four-year old boy who had drowned. Jimmy's mother told me that he was watching TV while she was working in the kitchen, but when she went to get him, he was nowhere to be found. After frantically looking for him, she called neighbors and the police, and an extensive search was started for the little boy.

At some point during all the confusion, she looked toward the little pond behind the house and realized that the lawn chair they kept by the side of the water's edge was gone.

Her husband would often come home from work and take Jimmy down to the pond. Holding him in his lap, they would fish. In that instant, she knew where her son was.

The edge of the pond was deep, but when she jumped into the water, she got him by his hair and pulled him out. Immediately after that, the lawn chair and fishing pole popped up to the surface of the water. It was later determined that Jimmy had gone to the pond and climbed into the lawn chair just like he had always done with his Daddy. He must have leaned forward, because the lawn chair had collapsed, trapping him, and he fell in the water.

His mother told me that the only way she had gotten through that awful time, was that she felt like she had somehow *rescued* her little son. She had been the one to find him. She told me that all during that dark time, God had been speaking to her heart. She and her husband visited several churches in the community before they found the one for them, and they were both wonderfully saved. After becoming actively involved in their church, they had a strong compassion for leading others to the Christ.

Eight years after Jimmy's death, Mark, his wife, and little daughter purchased the land across the street from Jimmy's family and built a house. Mark and Lisa were welcomed into the community by neighbors who brought them meals while they were getting settled. Friendships came easy, and they really enjoyed living there.

Their neighbors across the street kept inviting them to come to church, but they always had excuses as to why they could not go. But the neighbors never gave up! After several months, Mark and his family went with them to church. They heard the message of salvation for the first time and realized that it was what had been missing in their lives. They both responded to the invitation and received the Lord.

What a difference it made! The inner peace and joy they had been lacking was now an excitement they couldn't contain! They read about the Great Commission in the Bible, and they really believed it!

They began having Bible studies in their home, and aggressively began evangelizing their community.

They couldn't stop talking about what the Lord had done in their lives. They organized backyard barbecues so they could share the Gospel. They had folks over and told them about Jesus. They were new Christians, and they were on fire!

∽

A few months after his salvation, Mark began having pain in his legs. It became so severe that the doctors decided it must be more than muscle cramps or a pulled back, and they did some extensive testing. The results were devastating. Mark had cancer! It was everywhere! It was in his lungs, pancreas, liver, bones, and brain. There were a few futile attempts at chemotherapy, but his cancer had spread so rapidly. The doctors sent him home to die.

I was the hospice nurse assigned to care for him, and when I arrived at his home, I was amazed at how physically fit Mark looked. He had been a weightlifter, had a healthy lifestyle and he did not look like my typical cancer patient.

He was also very strong in his faith and witnessed to me that first day. He said that whether God healed him here on earth or healed him after he died, he figured he was a winner either way. Mark and Lisa were remarkably firm in their faith even though they had only been Christians for a few short months.

Mark had the opportunity to share the Gospel and the love of Christ with his extended family. On more than one occasion, I heard him telling them that salvation and the resulting peace and joy were what they had been looking for all their lives. Although he did not live to see the results, I know the seeds he planted with his loved ones will someday grow.

Something about Mark was amazing. The high doses of narcotics he was taking for pain caused him to hallucinate. He would talk incessantly about unrelated thoughts, and nothing made any sense. But at the end of my nursing visits when we would gather around his bed for family prayer, his wife would say, *"Mark, let's pray."*

He would immediately, in a strong, clear voice, pray the most beautiful prayer. He would pray for his family, that the Lord would take care of his wife and little daughter, and that God's will would be done in his life. Then he would express how much he loved the Lord.

Immediately after saying, *"Amen,"* he would return to his world of garbled speech and detached thoughts. I remember feeling the Lord's presence in his room so strongly during those times. Although I had heard of other patients who did that, Mark was my first experience with this. It was beautiful. It was sacred.

∽

Mark had a very large family, and they each had their own ideas about what should be done to *cure* Mark. Shark cartilage and tea made from plant roots were just some of the many things that they researched and felt compelled to try. But every day as Mark grew weaker, he was less responsive and more unwilling to try these experimental things. As a result, the family became divided. Some thought he should be forced to take everything in hopes of a cure, and some felt he should be allowed to die in his own way.

Many times, his wife, Lisa, would follow me out to my car and we would talk for a long time out there in the yard. Often, that was her only escape from the tension inside. She was resigned to his death but felt extreme pressure from some of his family members. I was supportive of her and reinforced what a good caregiver she was.

The hospice counselor spent a lot of time with the family, trying to get everyone to some middle ground. It was a difficult situation.

Mark had to be seen by a nurse every day. He was on IV chemotherapy drugs which were used to help shrink the tumors that were causing him so much pain. His care was very involved.

It was an hour's drive each way to his home, and my nursing visit usually lasted about two hours. I could count on a daily, four-hour ordeal. It drained me, both physically and emotionally.

～

Mark had been an engineer. Just months before his cancer was diagnosed, he had gone into business for himself. As a result, he was in that time period when he had no insurance coverage. His wife was not working, and this educated, middle-class little family had to file for Medicaid and food stamps to get through.

Mark worried about their finances and what his family would do when he was gone. But Lisa was always positive. She never complained. And if being on Medicaid embarrassed her, she never let it show.

She just kept on day after day, smiling and supporting her husband. I never once heard her question why this had happened.

～

Mark's family had all arrived and they stayed those last few days. They got motel rooms nearby because Mark's house was small and there were so many of them. One of his brothers usually stayed during the night to help with his care. Those last few days, Mark's medications had to be given around the clock, and Lisa was exhausted.

In the first weeks, little Rachel had loved climbing up in daddy's bed and *playing* with him. But toward the end, she was afraid. There was so much going on and she was much too young to understand.

Lisa's parents often took their granddaughter with them so Lisa could concentrate on taking care of Mark. But then Lisa felt guilty for being away from her.

～

When Mark died, it was a time of conflict for each family member. They were relieved that it was over, but at the same time, they felt guilty for feeling that way. The hospice counselor helped them realize that their feelings were normal and that it was okay to feel relief. She helped to reassure them that although they were relieved that Mark's suffering was over, they were saddened by their loss.

After the funeral home came, we counted and disposed of the narcotics and moved the equipment into the garage for pick up the next day. We tried to make the house look less like a hospital, and more like a warm, inviting home.

When I left, Lisa followed me out to the car, and we just held on to each other for a long time. I thanked her for the privilege of being Mark's nurse and reminded her that she had done absolutely everything that could be done for her husband. She told me that she had no regrets.

She said that she would not have made it without the help of the hospice staff and thanked me for my prayers and the friendship we had developed over those last months. I assured her that I would continue to pray for her.

At the funeral home visitation, the room was packed with friends, neighbors, and church folks. It was during that time that I talked with Mark's neighbor, and she told me her story. She said, "*If it had not been for my Jimmy's death, Mark might not be in heaven today.*" I was amazed by what had happened in the lives of so many people.

Mark had been the lead engineer on the construction of a beautiful resort hotel before his diagnosis. There were many employees from that project that were in attendance for his funeral. They formed a line from the back of the building to where the family was standing. And as they came forward to offer their condolences, they told us what Mark had meant to them.

A middle-aged man told us, "*Mark was such an encourager. My son was always in trouble, and I told Mark about it. He said nothing was going to work out if I didn't have Jesus. He helped me so much.*"

Another person shared, "*Mark convinced me that I could not raise all my children alone unless I had Jesus to help me. He was right! Things are working out really well with my family thanks to him.*"

An older man said, "*Mark caught me drunk on the job one day and sent me home. Then he came to my house and told me about Jesus. I got a good dose of Jesus right there in my house with my boss man praying for me. I'm a different man now.*"

A lady from the housekeeping department said to Lisa, "*Your husband changed my life. He led me to Jesus right there by the washing machines. I will never forget him. He was the best man I ever knew.*"

One by one they filed past the casket. They all had a story to tell. Stories of families that had been dysfunctional and broken until a man named Mark came into their lives and witnessed to them about the life-changing power of Jesus Christ.

∼

I look back at his story and remember how Mark and Lisa had been saved just a few months before his illness. They had been excited to share their salvation with their families and friends. That is how the Great Commission is supposed to work! Each of us must reach out to another person. And that person must reach out to someone else. And it continues on and on.

I often tell his story when I am in concert and I frequently hear, "I will never forget the story of Mark." He had an incredible testimony in his short life. He certainly inspired my life. Since knowing Mark, I have an even deeper compassion for people, and I am much more compelled to share the Gospel of Jesus Christ with others. We have all been commissioned to go and to tell. Babbie Mason's song, 'Each One, Reach One' is perfect for Mark's story.

Each One, Reach One

Today a man is somewhere proclaiming
the Good News.
Winning families to Jesus, all
around his neighborhood.
He tells them God is able to make their house a home.
He wants to win his world for Christ,
but He can't do it alone.

The message is unchanging, *"Go ye into all the world"*
And share the love of Jesus faraway or door to door.
You see, just like someone told you
that Jesus loves you so,
You must tell someone, who will tell someone
Until the whole world knows.

Each one can reach one.
As we follow after Christ, we all can lead one.
We can lead one to the Savior.
And together we can tell the world,
That Jesus is the Way,
If we each one, reach one.

Babbie Mason

CHAPTER 3

Please Hear Me, Shane

It is always heartbreaking to have a young patient who is dying. That was the case with Shane, a twenty-eight-year-old in a coma following a terrible motorcycle accident. As an alcoholic and drug addict, his lifestyle had him living on the edge.

He had been sent from the hospital to a rehab center where he could obtain care until arrangements could be made to have him moved to his home.

He was a handsome young man, tall and muscular, with piercing brown eyes. He had tattoos nearly everywhere on his body including tattoos of Satan, Nazi swastikas, and vulgar words. Although I talked to him throughout my initial nursing assessment, his eyes remained wide open but did not follow me. His stare was blank. He did not appear to be able to communicate in any way.

He was breathing on his own but had to have the assistance of an oxygen mask placed up to the tracheostomy opening in his neck. A feeding tube was going into his stomach. IV's infusing through a tiny catheter into his chest just below his collarbone and directly into his heart, helped keep him alive.

A catheter was draining his urine into a bag, and he was wearing a diaper because he had no control over his bowel function. Due to a raging infection, he was on several high-powered IV antibiotics. A fever left him soaking wet from head to toe. The rehab nursing staff had to change his gown and sheets repeatedly throughout the day.

～

But far more critical than Shane's physical condition were the family dynamics. His mother, on parole from prison, was upset that he wasn't sent directly home with her.

The continuous stream of family and friends at all hours of the day and night left the rehab staff exhausted. His visitors lacked good judgment when it came to helping Shane. A friend smuggled in a can of beer and attempted to give Shane *a good slug,* not realizing that his inability to swallow would cause him to gag and choke. That friend later stated, *"All Shane needs is some beer and a couple of hits of marijuana, and he'll be fine."*

Family members had insisted that he wear a Walkman so he could listen to music. When I realized that the music was hard rock, vulgar rap, and a litany of satanic statements, I asked them to remove it to prevent him from being so agitated. They replaced it with a TV that blared day and night.

～

Shane's visitors reeked of alcohol, cigarette smoke, and marijuana. Many of his friends were devil worshippers. The tattoos, body piercings, and occult paraphernalia were frightening to see.

His mother was caring and concerned, but she could rage at a moment's notice. She was determined to take him home so she could care for him there. She wanted him out of the rehab center, convinced that with loving support and in his home environment, he would someday just *wake up from his coma* and live a normal life again.

She did not want to hear about the damage to his heart or his brain. It made no difference to her when we tried to explain that he had been unconscious for an unknown length of time before a passerby initiated CPR. She didn't believe that this, coupled with a severe head injury had caused his brain damage and coma. She did not want to hear that his heart was critically damaged when he flipped over the handlebars and slammed into a tree. She was in total denial.

As the days passed the rehab staff fell in love with Shane. They teased him, hugged him, and chattered while performing his care. To our amazement, he began to follow us with his eyes. He did not always know where the sound of someone's voice was coming from, but he would move his eyes until someone walked into his field of vision.

At that point, he could make eye contact and maintain it for a little while. It was exciting for all of us to see the progress he was making, but at the same time, we knew his head injury and cardiac damage were irreversible.

All the diagnostic tests had told us that we were just waiting for his severely damaged heart to stop without any warning. This time, there would be no surviving it.

His heart muscle was already so badly damaged that it was barely pumping the blood through his circulatory system. There was also a strong probability of his developing pneumonia.

~

It was obvious to me from the first day that I met him, that Shane did not like me. I believe he could sense the presence of the Holy Spirit in me when I came into his room because he would become agitated. On the rare occasions that he made eye contact, I could feel his hate and hostility.

I would talk to him as I assessed him, suctioned his tracheostomy, or drew blood work. But there was a definite wall separating us and I couldn't get through it. I prayed for physical as well as spiritual protection every time I came into his room.

I could feel the very presence of evil.

~

After weeks in the rehab center, we finally acquiesced to the wishes of his mother and allowed her to have him taken by ambulance to her home. The tiny home was in a fairly isolated area, and it was a major effort to convert it into a mini hospital. With the hospital bed, oxygen equipment, suction equipment, feeding pumps, and boxes and boxes of supplies, there was not much room left for anyone to stand.

His mother was eager to learn how to care for him and she did a wonderful job. She learned how to turn and reposition him every two hours, how to perform range of motion exercises to help keep his muscles as flexible as possible, and how to feed and medicate him through his stomach tube.

She learned how to suction his tracheostomy, how to give him breathing treatments, how to drain and change the catheter bag, how to keep his diapers changed, and a myriad of other tasks. We provided all the help that we could.

A home health aide assisted with his daily care. The nurses saw him every day, and the counselor and chaplain were frequently there. But caring for him was a 24-hour, 7-day-a-week job, and his mother was exhausted and discouraged by the end of the first few days.

∽

I spent long hours with Shane's mother, and she developed trust in my judgment and advice. She cried on many occasions, as we discussed the inevitable outcome of the situation.

Although her personal religious beliefs included reincarnation, the use of crystals, and many other strange things, she often asked if I would pray with her. Although she verbalized confusion about her own beliefs, I never felt that I should talk to her about mine. I just supported her caregiving efforts. She cried uncontrollably every time I held her hands and prayed.

∽

Shane had not been on antibiotics since he left the rehab center, so when he developed a fever, the hospice doctor made a home visit. He sat down at the table with Shane's mother and me, and gently reinforced all the information she had been given previously: *no hope… just a matter of time…probably pneumonia now…*

How long did she want to put her son through all this? What would Shane's answer be if he could tell her whether to keep fighting or let him go?

She cried.

She realized that she was keeping him alive for herself, not for him.

She said, "He told me over and over again not to ever put him through anything like this. He said that he would never want to live if he couldn't function. He would hate me if he realized what we were doing to keep him alive."

Then she added, *"I'm glad his best friend Mike is in prison because they made a pact years ago that if something like this happened to one of them the other one would 'take him out.' But at least if Mike was here now, then I wouldn't have to make the decision."*

She cried and agonized over what she knew she should do. Then she refused the offer of antibiotics and any further attempts at treatment.

∼

Those last days were extremely difficult for his family and friends. At that point, his mother was the only one willing to let him go.

The other family members wanted him back again, *raising hell just like he used to.* After all, his mother had convinced everyone that when he got home, he would get well again and be perfectly fine!

It was chaotic.

People were all over the house, motorcycles all over the yard and in the street, dogs running in and out, people smoking on the back porch without closing the door, and the flies were everywhere.

Then there were the drugs.

We had been informed by a neighbor that this was the local drug house and that the police had been there regularly for the past few years. We didn't doubt it.

People came and went all hours of the day and night, reeking of alcohol and openly smoking marijuana.

I felt certain that other things were going on, but I did not actually see them.

∼

The day before he died, I spent many hours with Shane, trying to keep him as comfortable as possible and give his mother time to take a much-needed nap.

I do not know if he could hear or understand what I was saying, but I strongly felt the Lord leading me to present the Gospel to him that day. I made sure to talk about every step of salvation and prayed the sinner's prayer with the hope that he was understanding and accepting Jesus. I told him that without Jesus he was surely lost. I never saw any response in his eyes.

∼

We encouraged his mother to give him verbal permission to die. We told her how important it was to let him know that it was okay to let go.

That last night, she told me that she had climbed into his hospital bed, put her arms around him, and gave him permission to stop fighting. She said, "*Son, you have fought long enough. The doctors have done all there is to do. There is nothing more that I can do for you. I want you to just let go. It's time. I don't want you to fight this anymore. You need to let go because you will never get well."* She told me that he made eye contact with her and took a deep breath.

And then he died.

It seemed incredible to me that he had only been holding on to life for her, and that he was able to let go the moment she told him to.

∽

There was an eerie feeling in the house when I got there. His mother was strangely at peace and fiercely defended her decision to family members as to why she had chosen to let him go. There were many loud and ugly words spoken that day. Drugs and alcohol were being used in the backyard. The dogs were howling and trying to get up on the bed with Shane. The babies were crying. His grieving friends were racing their motorcycles up and down the dirt road, dust flying, and engines roaring as they screamed obscenities.

It was a hysterical nightmare!

I was so relieved that he was gone. It needed to be over. It had been over that day when he crashed his motorcycle into a tree and was lying unresponsive in the street. It had been over when he was rushed to the hospital by ambulance.

But it wasn't *really* over until his mother told him to let go. And when she did, it was *instantly* over. I want to think that he held on so that someone could talk to him about Jesus.

I often think about Shane and the lifestyle that he had. It was so foreign to anything I had ever known. It was difficult to show the compassion and love that came so naturally with my other patients.

But on that day, I trust that somewhere, in the dark shadows of his world, he heard me tell him about Jesus.

I trust that he understood. I trust that he was somehow able to ask for forgiveness of his sins and accept God's gift of eternal life.

I hope it wasn't too late.

Kaye Brinkman Howell

Chapter 4

Miss Emily's Secret

There is no one more gracious or sweet than a true Southern lady and Miss Emily surely fit the bill. She and her husband were sipping tea on their front porch, surrounded by beautiful plants and handcrafted items when I arrived to admit her to hospice.

Neither she nor her husband looked like they were in their nineties, but they had been married for more than seventy years!

She had been diagnosed with pancreatic cancer just two weeks before my first visit, and although they talked openly about her diagnosis, they were amazed at how suddenly this had happened.

Miss Emily had never been in the hospital in her entire life! She and Curtis both had enjoyed good health and a happy life together, and it wasn't until she began having significant pain in her abdomen that she finally gave in and went to see a doctor. The cancer had been diagnosed quickly, and at her age, she was not a candidate for treatment.

Everyone loved Miss Emily. She had company nearly every time I went to see her. Her house was filled with beautiful flower arrangements, cards, and food that her friends had brought to her. If I arrived for a nursing visit in the early afternoon, I could count on sitting on the porch and having tea with her, Curtis, and whatever special friends had dropped by.

On one of those visits, Curtis asked if I liked orange juice. When I said that I did, he went outside, picked several oranges from the tree, and squeezed them for a delicious glass of juice. Whether I wanted it or not, he had it ready for me from then on.

Miss Emily and Curtis loved to show off their crafts. Curtis had made some intricate and unique ships out of toothpicks. He had an entire collection! And there were beautiful, hand-made frames around his oil paintings. I was amazed at how professional his work was. He was also an inventor and held several patents. He was always working on some new gadget.

Miss Emily liked to crochet, needlepoint, cross-stitch, quilt, knit, and whatever else she could think of. Their home was so special. It was full of things that they had made and enjoyed together.

∽

Miss Emily lived for nearly a month after she was diagnosed. I was so glad for the opportunity to share her last days. She was one of the most optimistic, loving people I had ever cared for. I never heard her criticize anything or anyone. She had a quiet, gentle spirit that made you want to be around her.

From the first day, she called me her Special Angel. When I arrived at her home, the people visiting her would say, *"Oh, Emily. So, this is your Special Angel."*

∽

One day she told me a story about her mother. Many years before, Miss Emily had taken care of her invalid mother for ten years before her death. Her mother had suffered a stroke and was unable to speak. She had to feed her, turn her, and do everything for her.

Those years of care were more than a full-time job, but Miss Emily didn't mind. She loved her mother, and that was all that mattered. She would never have thought of placing her in a nursing home or hiring someone to take care of her.

But just a few days before her mother had died, she spoke! She had said, *"Emily, I hope when it's your time to go, you will have someone to take care of you just like you have taken care of me."*

Those were the only words she had spoken in years, and she never spoke again!

In relating her story to me, Miss Emily just clapped her hands, threw her arms around me, and said, *"And here you are!"* It made me feel very special.

Within two weeks, Miss Emily's skin had taken on the most brilliant orange color called jaundice. It was amazing to see her change so rapidly. At first, Miss Emily had very little pain and did not want to take medication. But as the days wore on, her pain increased, and we were able to keep her comfortable with the medications that she would allow us to give her.

She became weaker each day, but always had a smile for me. Although her skin was tremendously wrinkled and orange, she had a wonderful smile.

Miss Emily had her own teeth, and they were beautifully straight and pearly white. I remember thinking how unusual it was for a woman her age to have such pretty teeth.

∼

One day when I was making my usual nursing visit, she leaned back in her chair and very deliberately winked at me. After completing her examination, I leaned over and whispered, *"Do we have a secret?"*

She just beamed and said, *"Oh, yes! I know my mother sent you. She is looking down from heaven and she sent you here to take care of me. You are my Special Angel."*

Reaching into her sewing bag, she brought out a tiny porcelain angel pin. *"This is for you,"* she said. *"A Special Angel needs a special angel."*

She was so excited to be giving me a gift and was pleased that I immediately pinned it on my name badge. It is still there today! Every time someone mentions my angel pin, I remember Miss Emily and what she said.

After that day, she winked at me during every visit and said, *"I know that my mother sent you."* She was convinced of it!

∼

The day came when Miss Emily could no longer sit on her porch to sip tea and visit with friends. She had become so weak that I had a hospital bed delivered to her home. We had it placed in the living room, so that she could continue to be in the center of all the activity.

And there was a lot of activity! Once the word had spread that Miss Emily had taken a turn for the worst, her friends came every day. Lots of friends. Sometimes a whole house full of friends!

Miss Emily, amidst a sea of pillows, and in her best bathrobe, would visit with them, and offer tea and cookies, with Curtis assuming the role of the host. All the time, Miss Emily flashed her famous pearly white smile against the background of her orange face.

∽

Miss Emily decided that Curtis needed to learn to cook. Now you must realize that other than to squeeze my orange juice, Curtis had probably never even been *in* the kitchen in his lifetime!

His generation believed that men had no business being in the kitchen because their wives prepared the food and served them. That area was a woman's domain.

So you can just imagine the change of atmosphere the day I arrived to find poor Curtis, complete with a frilly apron, in the kitchen attempting to follow the directions Miss Emily called out to him from the living room. He was so concerned with messing up her kitchen that he would perform one task, then wipe down all the countertops and put everything back in place again. This routine continued until he had completed the recipe.

Miss Emily would chirp, *"Put the chicken breast in the pan."* Curtis would comply, then wipe down the countertops and straighten everything up.

"Sprinkle the seasoning salt over the chicken." Curtis would do so, wipe down the countertops, and put the seasoning salt back in the cabinet.

"Pour a little lemon juice over the chicken." He would pour, wipe down the countertops, and put the lemon juice back in the refrigerator.

He was still patiently following her instructions as I left that day. Whether he liked it or not, she was going to teach Curtis how to fend for himself in the kitchen.

Several days later, I nearly fainted when he presented a beautiful loaf of bread from the oven. He was so proud of himself! Homemade bread! Curtis was a success in the kitchen!

I never told him that I saw the wrapper for the frozen dough in the trash can. I just oohed and aahed over his expertise, and he smiled and kept his little secret to himself.

~

We had offered many avenues of assistance to Curtis, but he was determined to do everything himself. He was trying to take care of both himself and Miss Emily, not to mention his newly assumed kitchen duties.

Although I had spoken to their only daughter, Claire, by phone every few days to keep her updated about her mother's condition, she had been unable to travel due to her own serious health issues. I was very pleased that she was able to come that last week. She was a great help to her dad, and it was important to all of them that they were together.

～

By that time, Miss Emily was no longer flashing her beautiful smile. She was in and out of consciousness, and we had to watch carefully for signs of pain because she never would complain. We adjusted her medications as her facial expressions and moaning dictated.

Curtis refused to sleep in his bedroom those last three days. He slept in the recliner next to her hospital bed. He said to me, *"We have been side by side for over seventy years, and I'm not going to leave her now."*

It broke my heart to see him leaning over her bed, tears running down his cheeks and onto her face, as he tenderly caressed and kissed her. He constantly spoke of their love and how they had "never argued." They adored each other.

What a love story!

～

I was driving through their gate when Claire called to tell me that her mother had just slipped away. I tried to comfort Curtis, but he would continually return to her bedside and say, *"She isn't really gone, is she? She is just sleeping, isn't she?"*

He was inconsolable. He patted her face and hair. He straightened the neckline of her nightgown. He kissed her hands.

"My Emily, I don't know what I'll do without you," he said. And then he would repeat over and over, *"She isn't really gone, is she? She's just asleep, isn't she...?"*

He alternated between hugging Emily, Claire, and me. He just did not know what to do with himself.

We let him grieve. There was no rush to call the funeral home, so we just stayed around her bed for a long time.

The first neighbor that came by that morning was told the news, and she spread the word to their friends. We just waited. We wanted to give Curtis the time he needed.

About an hour after Miss Emily died, Curtis stood up as straight as his curved back would allow, and proclaimed, *"I'm going to get the mail."* He refused offers for someone to go with him.

He took a *very long time* to walk down that driveway to the mailbox.

∼

I received a letter from Curtis about a month after his beloved Emily died. This is what he had written.

My Dear Miss Kaye,
I've almost stopped crying over Emily, but it hasn't been easy.
Seventy years is a long time to be with someone you love.
I miss her so much. But at ninety-five years of age, it probably won't be long before I'll be up there with her.
When my time comes will you be MY Special Angel?
I'll have your orange juice ready.

Love from your forever friend,
Curtis

CHAPTER 5

Bobby's Promise

My young patient was only sixteen years old and was dying of cancer. I remember my apprehension about taking care of someone so young. What would I say to ease his sorrow? How would I handle the many questions that I anticipated he would ask?

The information I had been given about his situation made me realize this case would be a real challenge. I prayed for guidance as I drove to his home.

∼

Bobby's family life was in shambles. His mother had been killed in an accident a few years before, and he had been shuffled from one family member to another. No one wanted him. He was having a difficult time adjusting to school. He argued with everyone about everything. He lied. He stole. He would disappear for days at a time. No one understood what he was going through. He was never offered counseling.

Bobby had frequent stomach aches that began shortly after his mother's death. His family assumed it was because he was so nervous and upset over the tragedy. But when the pain got so bad, Bobby had begged to go to the hospital.

The diagnosis was colon cancer. It had already spread to other areas of his body. Surgery and a colostomy were next, and he began chemo and radiation therapy. He declined rapidly and his weight dropped to ninety pounds. The cancer was already so advanced that hospice was called in only four months after the initial diagnosis.

I had been told that the relatives he was living with at the time of his diagnosis said that they *couldn't handle cancer* and put him out on the street. He went to live with a friend and his mother. Miss Ruthie seemed to genuinely love and care for Bobby and assured him he would be comfortable and safe with them.

The courts agreed to let him stay there.

∼

Bobby may have been sixteen, but he looked more like a twelve-year-old. My heart melted when I first saw him. His eyes were hollow as he stared at me. He seemed fearful and withdrawn, sitting on the couch with his knees drawn up to his chest.

When I spoke to him, he told me that he was shy and didn't like to talk to strangers. He also said he was afraid of doctors and nurses. I said that I understood his feelings and that we would just visit so that we could get to know each other.

He had been through so much pain and fear, and I knew that for me to meet his needs, I must have his trust and confidence. I sat down in the chair across from him, kicked off my shoes, and tucked my feet up under me.

I asked if I could hold his little puppy named Spooky. I told him about Kassie, my Shih Tzu. I remarked about the program that he was watching on

TV, and we talked about his collection of baseball cards. I needed him to feel comfortable with me.

∼

I assured him that I would always be honest with him and that I would tell him everything he wanted to know. I said that I wasn't there to tell him what to do, but rather to help him get through this difficult time.

I told him I'd be coming every day and that I was so glad that he and I were going to be a team. The only remark I made about his health was to ask him if he was having any pain.

Before I left, I gave him my ministry card and said, "*This card is for you. It has my name and picture on it. I want you to remember that I am thinking about you when I am not here and that you and I are going to be friends. Before I come tomorrow, I'll call you to see if you want me to bring you a burger and some fries.*" His response was weak, "*Okay.*" That was the end of our first visit.

∼

The next day he let me examine him, but he didn't want me to look at his colostomy. I could only imagine the issues he was having with self-image, so I just asked if he was having any problems with it. That day we got his medications loaded into a weekly dosage box.

I made a big deal out of Spooky again and felt that this might be our point of connection. Bobby loved that little dog. It gave us something special to talk about. He talked a little more with me that day but was still very guarded.

On the third day, he let me bring him a hamburger and shake, and doggy treats for Spooky. He thanked me when I left. I prayed that we would be able to connect. By the end of that first week of visits, he allowed me to fully examine him.

We talked about how he felt, about pain control, and of course, Spooky. He was beginning to relax around me, and I really did enjoy the time I spent with him.

No one had told Bobby that he was dying. Miss Ruthie and I explained what was happening and how serious his situation was. He hung his head and said very slowly and softly,

"Well, okay then."

He seemed so detached from this awful reality. As time went on, I had the opportunity to talk to him about Jesus. Although he thought he might be saved, he wanted to pray with me. Our relationship changed after that day. He began to smile when I came in, and he wanted to hug me before I left.

One day he put his arms around me and wouldn't let go. He said that he was afraid to die. We talked about that for a long time. I assured him that when his special day came, he would not be in pain, that he wouldn't be afraid, and that he would just go to sleep and wake up in Jesus's arms. He just kept hanging on to my neck and began to cry.

"Promise me that you will be here when I die so I won't be afraid. Promise me."

His eyes were so desperate. I told him that only God knows when his special day would come, and I promised him that I would come just as fast as I could. He held on to me for a long time, and his tears ran down my neck.

∼

I felt a deep love for this child who had no mother. He had no one to hold him, no one to answer all his questions, and no one to be there for him. It had been easy for me to cross the emotional boundaries with him.

I was not only his nurse, but I had also become a kind of surrogate mother. I listened to his questions and answered them as best I could. I dried his tears. I listened when he reacted in anger to the lack of concern his relatives were exhibiting. I eased his physical pain with my medications. I nurtured him. And I genuinely loved him.

∼

Just a few days before he died, he asked me a surprising question. *"What did I do to make me die? I must have done something really bad. What did I do to make me die?"*

My tears came like a flood. In all of our talks over the previous months, in all of our conversations, in everything we had addressed, it had never occurred to me that he might think this was his fault.

This precious child had been carrying a load of guilt, thinking that something he had done had caused his illness and impending death!

I assured him that it was nothing that he did or didn't do, and I said it many times and in many ways.

With his eyes full of tears, he asked, *"Are you sure?"*

"Yes, I'm sure," I replied. *"Promise?"* he asked.

I hugged him tightly and said, *"I promise."*

~

His last few days were difficult. His tumor had invaded his spinal cord, causing compression, and he became paralyzed. He refused to be readmitted to the hospital. He refused more radiation therapy, which might have reversed the paralysis and made him more comfortable.

I believe he knew that the special day we had talked about was close and he wanted to stay at home. He was bedbound.

Spooky stayed between his knees or under his right arm. His pain was controlled, and he slipped in and out of consciousness.

During my visits, I held him in my arms and encouraged him to go be with Jesus.

~

Family members began to arrive. I had never counted so many aunts, uncles, cousins, and grandparents. I wondered where they had been these past few years! And from their tears and anguish, I believed that they were feeling the guilt of having abandoned this child.

I wanted them to feel guilty! I wanted them to feel his pain! I could not imagine how they could have been so indifferent!

I asked God to forgive them, but deep down, I did not mean it.

∼

I called to check on Bobby on Wednesday morning. He wanted to speak to me, so they put the phone up to his ear. I told him I was coming to see him in the afternoon.

"*Promise?*" he asked.

"*I promise,*" I answered.

"*I love you, Kaye.*" His speech was slurred from medications.

"*And I love you, too, sweetie,*" I replied.

"*Promise?*" was his expected response.

I answered, "*Oh, Bobby! I promise that I love you. You are my special, special boy. I will always love you.*"

With that, he drifted off to sleep. Just an hour before my scheduled visit, they called to tell me that he was gone. He had just slipped into the waiting arms of Jesus without fear and without pain. Spooky was licking his face when he took his last breath. We propped him up in bed and dressed him in his best T-shirt and favorite baseball cap.

∼

During my days with him, I had often wondered what might have happened if there had been stability and love in his life.

Would his physical complaints have been taken more seriously?

Could early medical intervention have mattered?
Would it have changed the outcome?
Did he ever really have a chance in life?
I cried for him and for what might have been.

I sang at his funeral. The little church was packed with friends and relatives. The pastor gave a strong evangelistic message, and I could feel the uneasiness of many people in the room. As I sat there, I looked at his picture surrounded by flowers on the communion table. The look in his eyes was so lost. So alone. So empty.

I prayed that somehow, I had made his last days more bearable.

I remember thinking about what possible good could come out of the death of a sixteen-year-old boy. But when I brought that to the Lord, He assured me that there was a reason.

"Promise, Lord?" I asked.

His comforting response was, *"I promise.*

CHAPTER 6

Granny Mama's Birthday

I first met Granny Mama in the hospital, where I went to admit her to hospice. She was a spunky little black lady with dancing eyes and a wide, toothless grin. She had experienced many things in her ninety-five years and was quite anxious to get out of the hospital and go home where she could get some good food. When I asked her what she wanted to eat, she said, *"Crackers and hog head cheese, and maybe a little piece of liver loaf."*

She said those were her favorites. I was secretly glad that I wouldn't be joining her for dinner.

Granny Mama was going to live out her last days with one of her daughters. Several of the family members were there in her hospital room, so I thought it would be a good time to see just what she knew about her condition. I asked her what the doctor had told her. She said, *"Well, I guess I got pneumonia, but he ain't never told me nothin."*

The family members just shrugged their shoulders and several of them said, *"We don't know either."* When I gently explained to Granny Mama that she had lung cancer, she flashed her eyes at me, then turned to two of her daughters.

"I told you I was sick. I told you I didn't have no cold. I knew it was somethin' bad. Humph! Y'all should have listened to me. I may be old, but I know what I'm talkin' about. I know when I'm bad sick."

No one said a word. Granny Mama crossed her arms across her chest, her fiery eyes darting from one person to another. One of her daughters said, *"Now, Granny Mama, don't you be talkin' like that. You know good and well that you wouldn't go see the doctor."*

Then she turned to me and said, *"And we wouldn't be here now if she hadn't passed out on us at the dinner table. We had to call the ambulance to get her here."*

Several family members mumbled, *"That's right,"* or *"uh huh."*

Granny Mama rolled her eyes toward the ceiling, pretending not to hear. The room got very quiet. After a little while, she said, *"Well, I'll just wait right here for Jesus to come get me. I'm ready. It's alright with me. I think I'll go now."*

After we convinced Granny Mama that we did not mean that Jesus was coming to get her *that very minute,* she agreed to go home with her family.

∽

Granny Mama had seventeen children, fifty-one grandchildren, seventy-five great-grandchildren, and thirty-five great-great-grandchildren. I mentally calculated that Granny Mama's family could fill up a small church!

When I asked her daughter about Granny Mama's name, she laughed and said, *"Well, she birthed her own young'uns and helped raise everyone else. So, we just all call her Granny Mama because that's who she is."*

They all had such sweet, loving spirits. Several of the men were preachers, and so were some of the women. And oh, how they could sing!

∽

I soon grew to love Granny Mama and her family. I enjoyed my nursing visits with them. And even though the little wooden house did not have air conditioning, they all seemed used to it. But I remember sweltering and often feeling faint from the heat. There was a single window air conditioner in Granny Mama's room, but it was never turned on.

I heard somewhere that women don't *sweat* but rather *glow*. Wrong! Oh, so wrong! Trust me, if I had never sweated before, I learned how to sweat while taking care of Granny Mama.

Soaked to the skin would be a more accurate statement!

Make-up would be running down my face and my hair seemed to be setting a world record for *strange*.

It was truly a humbling experience.

∽

Granny Mama decided that she wouldn't take any of her pills. I ordered them in liquid form. No way. We put the medicine in ice-cream or hid it in her pudding. Forget it. She was NOT going to take medicine. I have since wondered if we had added it to her beloved hog head cheese, if she could have tasted the difference. At any rate, she said she wasn't taking it. Period!

She didn't want to wear her oxygen because it bothered her. And she surely did not want to take a breathing treatment or anything else.

She was very much in charge!

She would say, *"I TOLD you that I'm waitin' for Jesus to come get me. I ain't takin' no medicine."*

∽

I spent a lot of time with her family. I was glad they were not trying to insist that she eat and take her medicines. Instead, they put the babies in bed with her and surrounded her with love and beautiful singing. Granny Mama was not in any pain, and she sang along to some of the old hymns.

People were always there. Family. Old and young. Granny Mama had raised not only her children but most of her grandchildren and great grandchildren as well. Many of the other women had done the same, so it was difficult to remember who belonged to whom. But it didn't seem to matter to them. They laughed and loved. They cooked and cleaned. They came and went.

There were very few tears. It was a sweet time.

∼

A few days before her 96th birthday, Granny Mama started talking to Jesus again. I heard her say, *"Jesus! Where are you at? I told you I'm ready! Come on! Come get me! Don't let me linger! Come on now! Take me home!"*

Her daughter told me that she had been talking like that all day. They kept encouraging her to wait until her birthday. *"Granny Mama, you got a birthday comin' in two days. We got to have a little party and lemon cake with ice cream. Then you can go. But you got to wait for your birthday."*

Every time I went to see her, people were gathered around her bed singing to her and reading the Bible. They were so positive and patient. The personal care aide who gave her baths, asked her, *"Granny Mama, are you going to go to heaven on your birthday?"* Granny Mama just smiled.

∼

Her birthday was a celebration for the entire family. The little house was packed. The yard was full. People were everywhere. They made her favorite lemon cake and homemade ice-cream. She was able to eat a little of it. They kept singing to her and reading special scriptures.

The entire time, Granny Mama was ignoring them and talking to Jesus.

"Jesus! Where are you at? I told you I'm ready! Come on! Take me home now! Jesus, are you listenin' to me? Don't You let me linger! You come get me! Do You hear me? Come on Jesus! Where are You at?"

I wish I could have stayed to see what happened. Her family told me that about 10:00 that night, she had still been having her conversation with the Lord.

They said that suddenly, she opened her eyes wide, and said, *"There You are! What took You so long? Let's go!"*

And with a smile on her face, she was gone. By the time I arrived, they were still singing. I could hear them before I turned into the yard. There were very few tears. She had lived a hard life, but it had been a good life, and she left a special, loving family behind. We all held hands and prayed. Then we sang *Happy Birthday* to her.

∼

I am not so sure that I would be as comfortable and bold in demanding that the Lord listen to me and that

He come and get me! But then, I'm not Granny Mama. She must have had a special hotline to heaven, because He heard her and personally came to escort her Home.

She closed the door to ninety-five hard working, faith-filled years, and received the best birthday gift of all… just what she wanted! An eternity with Jesus!

CHAPTER 7

Don't Let Me Die Like My Father

Fran knew that she was dying. She was losing the battle with cancer that had ravaged her body for years. She told me that professionals were like that. Fighters. She had been a successful attorney with an impressive record. Fiercely determined to win no matter what the odds, she was still bravely fighting. No longer in the courtroom, she was now in a battle for her life. The stakes were so much higher in this arena.

Fear in her eyes was the first thing I noticed when I met her.

She was already bedbound, but she was determined to control everything that she possibly could. She dictated just how her pillows were propped, exactly how many inches from the edge of the nightstand her glass of water would be placed, and which lotion she preferred for the home health aide to use on her skin on any given day.

But if the lotion didn't suit her, the aide had to bathe her again and change the lotion to something else. She wanted her bedroom door closed. No, open. Don't turn on that lamp, turn on this one. Not one click. Two. The room was not bright enough, so would we please open the drapes. The light had to be just right.

If she changed her mind about which nightgown to wear, it would have to be changed again. When she wanted to sit in the recliner, we would have to move everything and help her make the transition. But if she thought that she had better not try to sit up today, we would have to put her back in bed.

It was always something.

Everything seemed to be an issue. Almost everything in her life was now beyond her control, so she compensated by dictating and controlling every little detail in her bedroom.

Her family was used to her demands, but they were frustrated with the toll it was taking on everyone. Although verbal confrontations were few, the tension was obvious to anyone who came into the house.

~

Fran was an elitist. She had elevated herself above everyone and had drawn her family into feelings of superiority. The conversations that she had with her teenage children encouraged them to be snobs. After all, they were better than everyone. She verbalized it. She believed it.

Often when the nurse would arrive for a visit, she would direct the housekeeper to have her wait in the parlor until she was ready to see her. Depending on Fran's mood, the nurse might wait as long as an hour before being ushered into her presence.

Because of these many demands, she was not a popular patient with the staff.

I was her primary nurse, but I was not her first nurse. She had fired more staff from many different agencies than any of us could count. I'm not sure why she liked me, but she did. It worked to my advantage because I did not have to wait in the parlor.

~

Hospice nurses are often encouraged to wear street clothes, to make the patient feel less like being in a hospital and more like being at home. Fran liked my clothes. She had to know where I had purchased them and how much they had cost.

Often, she would say, *"I shouldn't be talking to you like this. I am a very private person, but I just feel comfortable with you. I feel like we connect, or something. Do you feel it too?"*

Fran knew the hospice philosophy, and she knew that she needed our care. But often, during our conversations, she would say, *"I don't think I'm dying yet. I mean, I've lived with this for years and I'm just not ready for the end."*

She was in denial one day and anger the next. Classic stages of grief.

~

For months, our conversations would include almost anything except spiritual matters. She had been quick to dismiss my inquiries in that direction. She believed in *something*, but not a living God or heaven or hell. She had lived a good life and had been a kind person, at least to most people.

But one day, she asked me, *"Do you consider yourself one of those born-again Christians? I mean, if it's not too personal a question. I just don't understand any of that. I go to church, but I am certainly not like you. You really believe in the heaven and hell thing and all that. I think I'm a spiritual person, but why are we so different? You seem so happy all the time, and so positive!"*

When I shared with her God's plan of salvation and how it brought about peace and joy, she decided that there were probably *many* ways to spirituality, and that certainly no particular one was better than another.

I shared special scripture passages with her and located them in her Bible. She would place a yellow sticky note to flag the page for future reference. She would not think of writing in her Bible, even though she thought it was just one of many ways to whatever there is in the afterlife, if there really is an afterlife.

As her body continued to fail, she wanted to talk a great deal about spiritual things. One day she was visibly upset upon my arrival. She told me that she had been thinking about her father. Her next words sent a chill over me.

She said, *"I was the only one in my father's hospital room when he died. He started screaming that the demons were dragging him into hell. He sat straight up in bed and said that he was going to hell and that it was too late. I can't stop thinking about that. That's a horrible memory. I do not want to die like that."*

I assured her that if we believe in God, and if we confess our sins, He will forgive our sins. I talked to her again at length about the plan of salvation and that we can *know* that we have eternal life. She asked me how she could get that knowledge. I directed her through the sinner's prayer, and she looked at me with tears in her eyes.

"*Is it really as simple as that?*" I told her that yes, it was just that simple. She said, "*My aunt had this real peace and assurance when she died. I want to be like that. I want to have that kind of peace.*"

I encouraged her to read her Bible and said that God would speak to her through His Word. I also suggested that every time she had an opportunity, that she should tell someone that she had accepted Jesus as her Savior.

∽

The next day, she seemed troubled. She said that she felt as though some little voice kept telling her that this wasn't real, that nothing had happened, and she was going to hell just like her father.

I explained to her how Satan worked and how he would just love to have her die as an unbeliever. I suggested that every time those thought came, that she thank God for saving her and forgiving her of her sins. I told her to speak it out loud so her ears could hear it. She was so unsure of her newfound faith that she wrote the words down in her notepad so she could quote them.

Although she had no idea how to talk to the Lord using her own words, she would repeat those few simple phrases and the Lord's Prayer throughout the day. Her faith grew stronger as she became bolder in her prayers.

∽

Getting past her fear of dying was another thing entirely. She was someone who had to be in control, *but she could not control her fear.*

We made that a special petition to the Lord.

Again, I led her through a series of statements that put her life in God's hands. I told her that the fear was from Satan and that she should not allow it to infringe on her newfound joy in salvation. I told her to deliberately, and with an act of her will, transfer the control from herself to Jesus. Again, she wrote down the words. Each day, as she grew more assured of what she was praying, she was gradually able to let the control go.

It took a very long time.

∽

The pain was another major fear that haunted her. A combination of years of suffering, a lowered pain threshold, and increasing pain as her tumor grew, required strong, highly concentrated medication that had to be increased as her pain escalated.

She was terrified that her pain would become out of control, and as she declined, her anxiety level increased. She begged me to move in with her so that I could be there for her day and night. Although her family had always had hired help around the clock, she still wanted me there.

∽

That kind of dependence on a hospice nurse has its positives and negatives. I was able to become very close to her during her last few months. She trusted me. Although I was not her only caregiver, she insisted on my input about every decision that was made by other staff regarding her care.

She had confidence in my judgment. She confided in me. We cried and prayed together. That kind of relationship is so intimate that often, even family members cannot share it.

The negative side to this degree of dependency is that she only wanted *me* to take care of her. She refused to talk with the chaplain, stating that she had nothing to say to him. She said she felt spiritually ready for the journey she was about to take.

She felt that the counselors were prying into her private life and the lives of her family. Although I explained that she would be leaving behind three teenagers who might need follow-up and counseling after her death, she denied that.

She said that her extended family would see to their needs.

~

Boundaries are issues that hospice personnel are faced with on a daily basis. The hospice philosophy stresses that each discipline, (nursing, personal care aide, chaplain, social worker or counselor, and volunteer) must set boundary limits based on their areas of expertise. The nurse should attend to the physical needs of the patient, the personal care aide assists with bathing, the chaplain deals with spiritual issues, volunteers often help with light housekeeping, and counselors direct and guide the totality of the family dynamics.

Most of the time this concept works well with a family. Sometimes it does not.

I know that nursing is my calling and that God is directing me in this path. And because I know that I have the promise of eternal life through Jesus Christ, I am compelled to share His Gospel. I do not want to stand before God and have someone say to me, "*You took care of me when I was dying. Why didn't you ever tell me about Jesus?*"

I strongly encourage the participation of the other disciplines, but occasionally a patient will bond strongly with one person, to the exclusion of others.

This is not the hospice way.

However, I believe that whatever it takes to meet the needs of my patients must be done. If I can personally share about Christ, that only makes me an extension of the arm of the chaplain. It does not replace him. I cannot meet the physical needs of my patients and ignore the most important issue they face:

Their eternal destiny!

In the end, Fran opted to die in the hospital, not in her home. She felt that she needed the security of having nurses around the clock, and I supported her decision. She confided in me just before the ambulance came, that she was afraid that her children might have difficulty knowing that their mother had died in her own bedroom. She said it was the only home they had ever known, and she was afraid it would hurt them.

I wished she had let the counselor become involved with her children because this is a typical issue that needs to be explored. She cried as they placed her on the stretcher, and then she asked that everyone leave the room except me.

She hugged me and said, "*I didn't want to die like my father died. You have shown me the Way, and I have found peace. You have been my friend. I realize that it won't be long, now, but I just can't go without thanking you for all you have done for me.*"

With tears and smiles, she was off to the hospital.

∼

Her husband kept in contact with me during the week, and one morning he called to tell me that she had died. I asked him how *he* was doing. He said that *she* had found peace, and that was the most important thing to him.

He said, "*She was such a fighter. She did not go easily, but she went peacefully.*

She told me to thank you again.

She said you would know just what she meant."

KAYE BRINKMAN HOWELL

CHAPTER 8

Angels on the Balcony

Cora came into my life in the fall of 1999 when I became her hospice nurse. She was sitting on the couch watching TV and her husband was at the kitchen table. Their beautiful log home was filled with collections of hand decorated plates, quilts, and collections of antiques. Their yard was immaculate with huge shady trees, and a peaceful little stone waterfall that was surrounded with beautiful flowers. It looked like a picture you would see in a book.

∽

Back in 1981, Cora had been diagnosed with cancer. After surgery, chemotherapy and radiation therapy, she had been given a clean bill of health. But in 1988 cancer had been found again. That time one of her kidneys was involved and had to be removed. Through all of that, she had held tightly to God's hand. She had given her life to the Lord as a young girl, and had never wavered. She had always been strong in her faith.

∽

Several years after Cora's diagnosis, her oldest daughter had been diagnosed with cancer. Sadly, she had lost her battle after years of treatment. Although Cora and her family had been devastated, they had a deep sense of peace.

∼

When Cora began having severe pain in her back and abdomen, the news had not been good. The surgeon explained that cancer had invaded her remaining kidney and had spread to her surrounding organs. He had told Cora that it was too extensive for surgery, and that even chemo and radiation would not help. At that point I was assigned as her hospice nurse. Many times, when I meet patients and their families, I know immediately that they are going to play a special role in my life. Something just clicks and there is a bond from the beginning. That was the way I felt with Cora.

∼

Cora was so weak and sick that she spent most of her days on the couch. Her daughters took turns staying with her at night to help their dad care for her. Cora felt that she would die before Christmas, and her family, seeing her suffering, agreed that she might.

But after weeks of symptom treatment, her pain was under control and she felt like putting on her make-up and getting out of the house. Her energy level increased, and she was excited to be feeling better.

∼

When I made my nursing visits, Cora always wanted us to pray together. She said that she was trusting in the Lord to heal her, because she had so many things yet to do in her life. She wanted to see her granddaughters married. And she wanted to continue to be involved in her church's outreach program which provided counseling to troubled women. She had developed a close relationship with many of those women who were living in shelters and she felt that by sharing her cancer journey with them, that she might give them courage and hope.

But most of all, she told me that she wanted God's will in her life, *even if* that meant that He would not heal her here on earth. She wanted God to use her to make a difference in the lives of other people. She believed that He would use her either through her life or through her death. She talked a lot about faith. Faith is believing something even though you cannot actually see it. She told me that faith was like blind trust: you believe, so you hang on. She would say, "You just have to keep holding on to God no matter what."

∽

Cora's husband was having medical problems of his own, with a heart condition and diabetes. But through it all, neither one of them faltered. I had never before seen people with the level of faith that they had.

∽

Just after Christmas, Cora and her husband took a weekend getaway. Something happened to their relationship that weekend. She told me later that it was as though they had fallen in love all over again. Starting that weekend, they would wake up very early every morning and they would talk and pray together. Then they would fall asleep again in each other's arms. They told me that those final months were the best of their lives. They found closeness and love like they had never experienced.

Several weeks before she died, the family went through another crisis. Their granddaughter was involved in a serious car accident and was in critical condition. For several days it was not known if she would survive.

But Cora and Jack knew just what to do. They had been through many difficult times, and together, they prayed for a miracle. Their church family was praying, and the request had been placed with an international prayer chain.

During my next visit to Cora, she and Jack were praising the Lord that their granddaughter had come out of her coma and was soon to be discharged home.

They knew the Lord had performed this miracle!

~

As Cora's condition began to deteriorate, I visited her daily, adjusting the medications to keep her comfortable. She always wanted me to pray with her before I left, and she would hug me tightly and tell me how much she loved me. Family members were always there, and our tears flowed freely. She was such a special lady. I knew that I would really miss her.

~

A week before she died, she told me that she had been lying on the couch when a group of angels had appeared and stood on her balcony. She gestured to me where they had been standing.

"*They come back every day,*" she said. "*They just look at me. But I want to go with them. I want them to take me with them.*" Her voice was pleading.

I replied, "*Cora, talk to them and tell them that you are ready to go.*"

She drifted off to sleep as she whispered, "*Come back. Please come back.*"

∼

She was in and out of consciousness that last week.

On Sunday evening, with her family gathered around her, she took her final breath. I believe that her balcony angels returned to escort her into the loving arms of Jesus.

What a woman of faith! I was so blessed to know her. One of her favorite songs was 'Peace in the Midst of the Storm,' and she had lived her life that way. The words of that song seemed written just for her.

Peace in the Midst of the Storm

When the world that I've been living
in crumbles at my feet.
And when my life is all tattered and torn,
Though I'm wind-swept and battered,
I'll still cling to His cross.
He gives me peace in the midst of the storm.

∼

When I come to the end of my journey,
and life's final picture is taking form,
In the darkness of my suffering a light
comes shining through.
He gives me peace in the midst of the storm.

∼

He gives me peace in the midst of
my storm tossed life.
He's my anchor, He's my rock to
build my faith upon.
Jesus Christ is my refuge and
I fear no alarm.
He gives me peace in the midst of the storm.

Stephen R. Adams

Chapter 9

When Jenny Sang

One of my most memorable hospice patients was Jenny, a ninety-year-old widow who lived in a huge, sprawling old house in the country. The warm, homey feeling there reminded me of my grandmother's house. A huge porch ran across the front of the house and down one side. It had a squeaky wooden swing and comfortable chairs that promised relief from the hot summer sun. I well remember the hardwood floors in every room that had to be swept daily.

Like most newlyweds of her day, Jenny and her husband had proudly furnished their home with what, over the years, became antiques. Even the heavy damask drapes spoke of earlier times and gave a musty odor to the living room that even open windows could not dispel.

~

Jenny had been active in her community and church. The walls of her home were covered with pictures of family members and memorabilia from years past.

There was the special Mother's Day award, where Jenny had been recognized as the mother with the most number of children present in church that day, and many more. She had been designated as the Most Valuable Choir Member, President of the Ladies'

Ministries, Missions Director, and Bible Teacher of the Year. Then there were the county fair awards. She had awards for her pies, cakes, pickles, jellies, and soups.

Whatever needed to be done in the church or community Jenny had done it, and over time, as awards were passed out, she had received them all. There she stood, always in her little hat, a huge purse in the crook of her left arm and her King James Bible in her left hand, held against her heart. Always tall and incredibly thin, she looked the same year after year.

∽

Jenny's husband had died some 30 years before and although children and grandchildren lived just minutes away, she wanted her independence. About seven years before I became her hospice nurse, she had suffered a major stroke that left her paralyzed and unable to speak.

Her family hired a caregiver to live with her, someone who would see to her every need. Lucy had lived there with Jenny ever since, and the love they shared made her seem like a member of the family.

Jenny could do nothing by herself. After being bathed and dressed each morning, she would be lovingly moved to the recliner. She gave no sign of being able to comprehend what was going on around her. She just lay peacefully in whatever position she was placed.

∽

On my initial nursing visit, I was greeted by Jenny's son, who insisted that I sit at the kitchen table with him and have a glass of iced tea. He wanted to give me a bit of history about her and the family. He expressed concern that his mother not suffer, but was glad that her doctor had asked hospice to come in. I assured him that we would give her our best care.

The most remarkable thing about Jenny was that although she could not speak a word, she could sing *every verse* to any old church hymn you could name. Lucy would start to sing, and Jenny would join in with a clear, high voice. I had heard about this amazing phenomenon but had never personally experienced it until Jenny came into my life. I still find it a mystery.

Even though a stroke can remove rational thought and the ability to speak, there sometimes remains a secret door that music can open. Such was the case with Jenny. Sometimes I would deliberately choose a song that I thought she probably wouldn't know, but she would pick it up halfway through the first verse. I never did find a hymn that she did not know, but it was fun trying.

When Jenny died, some of those old songs seemed to die with her. We don't hear them much anymore, but those hymns had guided her life.

'My hope is built on nothing less than Jesus' blood and righteousness'
had long ago established her feet on the Solid Rock.

'Blessed assurance, Jesus is mine'
echoed the dedication she felt to God's will.

'O, for a thousand tongues to sing'
Jenny had only one, but oh, could she sing her Redeemer's praise.

'Rock of ages, cleft for me, let me hide myself in Thee'
She had always taken refuge in the safety of His protection.

'So, I'll cherish the old rugged cross, 'til my trophies, at last, I lay down'
I do not think that Jenny's humble nature would have allowed her to claim trophies, but I feel sure that heaven has a record of all the lives she has touched. Mine is one of them.

'Amazing grace, how sweet the sound, that saved a wretch like me'
*God's amazing grace had changed her life.
It still changes lives today for anyone who asks!*

I suppose my favorite of all the hymns we sang together, was 'When the roll is called up yonder, I'll be there.' Maybe it was because her facial expression seemed to change every time we sang it. Maybe it just blessed my heart to hear her sweet voice. Maybe it was because her eyes would always fill with tears as we sang that first verse. I do not know. But for a brief moment, I believe that those words reached deep into the quiet places of her spirit as Jesus gently reminded her that she had not been forgotten and that her name was still on His roll.

Today, every time I hear one of those old songs, my mind goes back to Jenny and the way she held fast to her Savior's strong and mighty hand.

I added her favorite hymns to this story because the words, so beautifully written in old English, are so powerful.

Thank you, Lord, that Jenny's life was such a testimony. May I be as faithful.

When the Roll is Called up Yonder

When the trumpet of the Lord shall sound
and time shall be no more
and the morning breaks eternal, bright, and fair
When the saved of earth shall gather
over on the other shore
and the roll is called up yonder, I'll be there.

∼

On that bright and cloudless morning
when the dead in Christ shall rise,
and the glory of His resurrection share.
When His chosen ones shall gather
to their home beyond the skies
and the roll is called up yonder, I'll be there.

∼

Let us labor for the Master
from the dawn 'till setting sun.
Let us talk of all His wondrous love and care.
Then when all of life is over
and our work on earth is done
and the roll is called up yonder, I'll be there.

∼

When the roll is called up yonder
When the roll is called up yonder
When the roll is called up yonder
When the roll is called up yonder, I'll be there.

James M. Black

The Solid Rock

My hope is built on nothing less
than Jesus' blood and righteousness;
I dare not trust the sweetest frame
but wholly lean on Jesus' name.

∼

When darkness seems to hide His face,
I rest on His unchanging grace.
In every high and stormy gale,
my anchor holds within the veil.

∼

His oath, His covenant, His blood
support me in the whelming flood.
When all around my soul gives way,
He then is all my hope and stay.

∼

When He shall come with trumpet sound,
oh, may I then in Him be found.
Dressed in His righteousness alone,
faultless to stand before the throne.

∼

On Christ, the solid Rock I stand
All other ground is sinking sand
All other ground is sinking sand.

Edward Mote

Blessed Assurance

Blessed assurance, Jesus is mine!
Oh, what a foretaste of glory divine!
Heir of salvation, purchase of God,
born of His Spirit, washed in His blood.

∽

Perfect submission, perfect delight,
visions of rapture now burst on my sight.
Angels descending bring from above,
echoes of mercy, whispers of love.

∽

Perfect submission, all is at rest.
I in my Savior am happy and blest.
Watching and waiting, looking above,
filled with His goodness, lost in His love.

∽

This is my story, this is my song
Praising my Savior all the day long.
This is my story, this is my song
Praising my Savior all the day long.

Fanny J. Crosby

Rock of Ages

Rock of Ages, cleft for me,
let me hide myself in Thee.
Let the water and the blood,
from Thy wounded side which flowed,
Be of sin the double cure.
Save from wrath and make me pure.

∼

Not the labors of my hands
can fulfill Thy law's demands.
Those for sin could not atone.
Thou must save and Thou alone.
In my hand no price I bring.
Simply to Thy cross I cling.

∼

While I draw this fleeting breath,
when mine eyes shall close in death.
When I rise to worlds unknown
and behold Thee on Thy throne.
Rock of Ages, cleft for me,
let me hide myself in Thee

Augustus M. Toplady

The Old Rugged Cross

On a hill far away stood an old rugged cross, the
emblem of suffering and shame.
And I love that old cross where the dearest and best
for a world of lost sinners was slain.

∼

Oh, that old rugged cross, so despised by the world
has a wondrous attraction for me.
For the dear Lamb of God left His glory above
to bear it to dark Calvary.

∼

In the old rugged cross, stained with blood so divine,
such a wonderful beauty I see.
For 'twas on that old cross, Jesus suffered and died
to pardon and sanctify me.

∼

To the old rugged cross, I will ever be true
Its shame and reproach gladly bear.
Then He'll call me someday to my home far away,
Where His glory forever I'll share

∼

So I'll cherish the old rugged cross,
Till my trophies at last I lay down.
I will cling to the old rugged cross,
and exchange it someday for a crown.

George Bennard

Amazing Grace

Amazing grace! How sweet the sound,
that saved a wretch like me!
I once was lost, but now I'm found.
Was blind, but now I see.

～

'Twas grace that taught my heart to fear,
and grace my fears relieved.
How precious did that grace appear,
the hour I first believed.

～

Thro' many dangers, toils and snares,
I have already come.
'Tis grace hath brought me safe thus far,
and grace will lead me home.

～

The Lord has promised good to me,
His word my hope secures.
He will my shield and portion be
as long as life endures

～

When we've been there ten thousand years,
bright shining as the sun,
We've no less days to sing God's praise
than when we've first begun.

John Newton

The Hallelujah Side

Once a sinner far from Jesus,
I was perishing with cold.
But the blessed savior heard me when I cried.
Then He threw His robe around me,
and He led me to His fold.
Now I'm living on the hallelujah side.

~

Tho' the world may sweep around me
with her dazzle and her dreams,
Yet I envy not her vanities and pride.
For my soul looks up to heaven
where the golden sunlight gleams.
And I'm living on the hallelujah side.

~

Nor for all earth's golden millions
would I leave this precious place,
Tho' the tempter to persuade me oft' has tried.
For I'm safe in God's pavilion,
happy in His love and grace.
And I'm living on the hallelujah side.

~

Here the sun is always shining;
here the sky is always bright.
Tis' no place for gloomy Christians to abide.
For my soul is filled with music
and my heart with great delight,
And I'm living on the hallelujah side.

~

And upon the streets of glory
when we reach the other shore,
And have safely crossed the Jordon's rolling tide,
You will find me shouting
"Glory" just outside my mansion door,
Where I'm living on the hallelujah side.

∾

Oh, glory be to Jesus! Let the hallelujahs roll!
Help me ring the Savior's praises far and wide.
For I've opened up toward heaven
all the windows of my soul.
And I'm living on the hallelujah side

J. Howard Entwisle

Kaye Brinkman Howell

O For a Thousand Tongues to Sing

O for a thousand tongues to sing
my great Redeemer's praise.
The glories of my God and King,
the triumphs of His grace!

∼

My gracious Master and my God,
assist me to proclaim
to spread through all the earth abroad,
the honors of Thy name.

∼

Jesus, the name that calms my fears,
that bids my sorrows cease
'Tis music in the sinner's ears,
'tis life and health and peace.

∼

He breaks the power of canceled sin,
Hs sets the prisoner free.
His blood can make the foulest clean,
His blood availed for me.

Charles Wesley

CHAPTER 10

A Second Chance

Her story was so very tragic. Tina was the product of a broken home. Disillusioned and defiant, she got pregnant at seventeen and moved to the west coast with the father of her baby. She developed a drug habit, and prostitution was her only means of paying for the drugs that she continued to desperately need.

Her baby, Kasey, was often left alone in her crib, until her mother returned, stoned and sick. As the years went by, Tina's habit became stronger, and Kasey was shuffled from friend to friend while her mother disappeared into the night with one man and then another.

Child welfare had tried on many occasions to take Kasey into protective custody, but Tina always managed to disappear with her again before that could happen.

∼

Tina acquired HIV from one of her many contacts. Although estranged from her family, she called her mother for help. Beverly, a new Christian, eagerly went. Tina had never known her mother as a born-again Christian. During Tina's childhood, her mother had wanted nothing to do with God.

Beverly was desperate for one more chance and prayed that this would be the time she could influence her daughter. Perhaps this was the time

Tina could come to know Jesus. But the visit was a disaster. Although she was in full-blown AIDS by then, Tina continued her prostitution to pay for her drugs.

Beverly tried to get Kasey away from that environment, but Tina's many addicted friends moved the child again. One night in a drunken, drug-induced rage, Tina physically attacked her mother and beat her so severely that Beverly spent several days recovering in the hospital. In a move of desperation, she pressed charges against her daughter and a warrant was issued.

Again, Tina was nowhere to be found. Beverly returned home and continued her prayer vigil for her daughter and grandchild.

∽

When Kasey was six years old, Tina called her father and asked if she could come to live with him. She needed increasing medical attention and help with Kasey. But more than anything, she did *not* want her mother to know that she had come home. She wanted nothing to do with her mother, and she certainly did not want to hear one more word about Jesus.

By then, Tina's father was living with his fifth wife. Although his wife was wary, they gave Tina permission to come to live with them. She packed her belongings in a single suitcase, and with her daughter, Kasey, and two Labradors, had a friend drive them to her dad's home in Florida.

∽

Her father's tiny home was in a very bad neighborhood. A chain-link fence around the property could not hide the yard that was filled with broken-down appliances and old cars. Someone had to come and open the gate to keep the dogs from attacking me every time I arrived for Tina's care. The wooden porch was rotting away, and it was risky just walking up the steps.

The inside of the house was unbelievable. I had never encountered such filth. The kitchen was piled high with stinking garbage. An old sofa was broken down and covered with cigarette burns. The only curtain in the house was hanging and torn; the other windows were either bare or covered with sheets and old newspapers.

I found Tina in a small bedroom lying on a filthy mattress that was flat on the floor and had no sheets. Her suitcase, scattered clothes, and Kasey's toys were on the mattress with her. There was no place for me to sit, much less to set up my supplies to take care of her.

At sixty pounds, Tina looked like a skeleton. AIDS had ravaged her body, and she was covered with open sores from the Kaposi's sarcoma that AIDS patients often develop. I counted thirteen earrings in her ears, and many tattoos on her body.

She wore an ankle bracelet of gold skeletal heads, and she was chain-smoking marijuana. Her dentures looked oddly out of place. They were so large for her mouth, that it was obvious her weight loss had been severe.

∽

Her daughter, Kasey, was one of the most beautiful little girls I had ever seen. Long, thick, blonde hair cascaded down her back and her blue eyes sparkled. Amazingly intelligent for the circumstances she had been in, she had a quick wit and could carry on conversations with adults on their level.

It dawned on me that she had not been around other children.

She was smiling and friendly. The love that she and her mother shared was obvious. Kasey knew that her mother was sick. Tina had told her that it was cancer, so there was never any discussion about AIDS in her presence. She was excited that a nurse was coming to the house to help her mom get well.

I wondered how we would handle all of that when the time came.

∽

Tina had no income, and she had no money for an emergency. She obtained her cigarettes and marijuana from her father, who was having a hard time saying, "*no*" to his dying child.

Just after Thanksgiving, Tina rallied somewhat and started talking about explaining to Kasey that she was going to die. She wanted privacy for this discussion and told me that Kasey liked seafood. I gave her money for their meal and her father provided transportation to and from the restaurant.

I do not know what Tina told Kasey that day, but Kasey never indicated that anything was different.

∽

As we had expected, it was not long before Tina's stepmother resented the intrusion into her home. On more than one occasion, the police were dispatched to settle the domestic fighting in that family.

When her stepmother said, *"Either Tina goes or I go,"* Tina called her mother for help. Beverly did not even know that Tina was in Florida but quickly came to pick her up and take her to live with her across town.

Tina inadvertently left some of her medications and several personal items behind, but when I called her father regarding them, he refused to let her come back to get anything. He was furious that she had chosen her mother over him!

He installed a new padlock on the gate and left her medicines hanging on the fence.

Then he threw the remainder of her things in the ditch between the gate and the road, saying he never wanted to speak to her again.

By Christmas, Tina was rapidly going downhill. During her conscious moments, she was anxious about who would take care of Kasey. An attorney came to the house and drew up legal papers for Beverly to have custody. Two days later, Tina and her mom had another fight and Tina wanted her father to have custody. He refused to even talk about it.

It was a constant tug-of-war over Kasey and I wondered what the outcome would be. Tina pawned her gold ankle bracelet to buy Kasey a Christmas gift. Kasey gave her mother a piece of construction paper covered with glitter and glue. It was a picture of a

Christmas tree with a huge, oversized angel on top. An arrow pointed to the angel with the words, *my mom is an angel* written across it.

They taped it to the wall beside Tina's bed.

∼

Beverly and I had prayed together on so many occasions, hoping that something we could say or do would influence Tina for the Lord. Thankfully, just a few days before she died, Tina prayed for forgiveness of her sins and surrendered her heart and life to Jesus Christ. She was very unemotional about it, but her mother and I were elated. Beverly literally danced me across the room when she told me the good news.

Although Tina often called for her father to come during her last hours, he refused. He told us that she had chosen her mother over him, and he didn't want anything else to do with her.

Even with their family dynamics in shambles, I still couldn't believe that he would refuse her dying request. I wonder now if he ever thinks about what he missed those last days. I wonder how he could not be there for Kasey.

∼

Tina took her last breath one afternoon just before I arrived for her nursing visit. Kasey and both the dogs were in the bed with her. The house was totally quiet.

Beverly and I talked to Kasey about how her mama had accepted Jesus as her Savior and was now in heaven. Strangely, she was unmoved. I never saw her shed a tear.

I think of Kasey now and then. I trust that her early years of neglect, having a mother who was a drug addict and prostitute, and all the fear, uncertainty, and deep scars that must have come with that whole package, can be overshadowed by the love of her Christian grandmother who obtained her custody. I am glad they both got a second chance.

Kaye Brinkman Howell

Chapter 11

Home for Christmas

Harry had not always been a respectable man. He spent most of his life drinking away the money that he brought home from the phosphate mines. Rough and uneducated, he never missed an opportunity to give someone a good tongue-lashing. His reputation as a fighter was well-known, and people knew better than to cross him.

Sunday was Harry's favorite day. Getting up early, he would leave the house without a shower or shave, and with his fishing gear and a cooler of beer, he would connect the little boat to his old truck and go to the river to spend time with his buddies. Most of them were like Harry, hard working family men who liked to drink beer and go fishing. By day's end, he would stagger home, dirty and drunk, but hopefully, with a line of fish to clean and put in the freezer.

He was a gruff old man. His first wife had died when his children were in elementary school, and he never forgave her for leaving him like that. She had been the love of his life.

To make matters worse, their only daughter looked exactly like her mother, and was a constant reminder of happier days. Because of that, Harry could never bring himself to show her any affection, and she grew up thinking that he didn't love her. Those early scars would remain for a lifetime.

The boys, on the other hand, received all his attention. As they grew up, they went fishing with their dad. Although Harry knew what the law said about underage drinking, he wasn't about to let that stop him from teaching his boys how good a cold beer was on a hot day.

It wasn't long before the oldest boy began getting in trouble at school, cutting classes and drinking. The younger boy was a bit shy and had always been afraid of his father. All that would change later, but during their teen years, life was difficult.

∼

Harry met a good Christian woman named Bernice. She was working as a cashier at the local Walmart, and before long, Harry took a liking to her. She had a couple boys, and they were really decent kids. They went to church with their mother every Sunday. She insisted that they keep up their schoolwork, and made sure that they had clean clothes to wear every day.

Bernice told Harry that she could never marry an alcoholic, so he cleaned up his act for a few weeks, attended church with her and spent Sunday afternoons with her and the children. His ploy worked, and before long, they were married.

Exactly two weeks after the wedding, Harry was back to his old antics again, drinking beer and spending Sundays fishing. Bernice was too proud and hurt to leave him, so she took her boys to church as she had always done and held her head high. Harry's daughter gladly went with them. It was better than spending the day alone while her dad and brothers did their usual Sunday thing.

∼

Years went by and very little changed. Bernice's boys eventually joined the Army, married, and had families of their own. Harry's boys lived hard, drank hard, and went through a series of jobs, and almost as many marriages. Harry's daughter, Louise, married a good, hard-working man and lived just a few miles from her father and stepmother.

Although Bernice loved Harry, she didn't approve of his lifestyle. But she resigned herself to being satisfied with the way things were, and tried to stop wishing that he would change. Harry was Harry. He was faithful to her, and she knew that he loved her deeply, but that was where their similarities ended.

Bernice continued to be involved in her church. She sang in the choir, was active with the ladies' group, and was there every time the church doors were open. Her church was her life and all her activities revolved around it.

∼

The years passed. Harry's boys settled down and raised their own families nearby. Louise was even able to forgive her dad for his attitude toward her when she was a child. Bernice's boys finished their tours of duty with the Army and returned home.

Everyone lived within a few miles of each other, and they all got along well. Family disagreements were rare, and there was a lot of respect for both

Harry and Bernice. The children loved them both and knew that Bernice had brought real stability to the family. And there was never a question about the love that Harry and Bernice shared for each other.

One Sunday, one of Harry's former co-workers from the mine, showed up in the afternoon to join them in fishing. Harry really liked Sonny. They had both retired at the same time and they had some great stories to share. But Sonny could not be convinced to drink with them, nor to come earlier in the day.

He was a *churchgoer* and only came to the river after the morning worship service and a good Sunday dinner with his family. But he was such a likable guy that Harry found himself really getting to know him.

One afternoon when Harry and Sonny were alone in Harry's boat, Sonny began to talk about Jesus. For the first time in his life, Harry didn't bristle and change the conversation. He listened to the testimony of a man whose life had been changed by the saving grace of Jesus Christ.

Bernice remembered that Sunday afternoon when Harry came home early and went straight to the shower. A little while later, he reappeared in the living room, clean, shaved, sober and calm. He told her how he had asked Jesus to forgive his sins and to take control of his life. He said that he was a new man and that he had never felt better. They both began crying and fell into each other's arms.

The story of how Harry met Jesus down at the river traveled through their community almost as quickly as it had happened. Harry went to church that night and made a public profession of faith. Then he went home and poured out all his beer.

Things were never the same after that day. Harry still loved fishing, but only *after* church and family dinner. He would show up at the river in the afternoon, but instead of drinking, he spent his time fishing and talking to his old buddies about Jesus.

~

Seeing the change in Harry's life and wanting that kind of peace in their own lives, several friends were saved. Harry was making a new impact at the river; not at all like the impact he had once made.

Bernice's boys, both strong Christians and in loving families, were overjoyed. This is what they had been praying for!

Harry's boys, at first skeptical of the change in their old dad, soon were asking about what *they* needed to do to be saved.

~

In the Fall, Harry began having some severe pain in his chest and started coughing up blood. Years of cigarette smoking had taken their toll, so he wasn't really surprised when the doctor told him he had lung cancer. Because of his many other health issues, he chose not to take chemo treatments. The doctor sent him home where hospice care would keep him comfortable during his last days.

Harry and Bernice both witnessed to me that day in their home when I admitted him to hospice. Harry had to tell me his story and I rejoiced with them as they told me what a difference it had made in their lives. I met their children, grandchildren, and many of their friends. Harry was loved by so many people.

His health deteriorated quickly, and he went into a coma just a few weeks before he died. One day, as I was taking care of him, I heard him praying. It was just a phrase here and there, but I knew what he was saying.

"Lord, please take me home for Christmas."

The November days came and went, the weather turned, and Harry was still with us. December, with all the excitement and joy of the approaching holiday season, was suddenly upon us and I wondered if Harry would make it home to heaven by Christmas.

Bernice decided not to put up a tree that year, and she wasn't much in the mood for cooking. She spent most of her days with Harry, and answering the many phone calls from folks who were checking on him.

Friends came by every day with meals for the family and any visiting guests. My nursing visits indicated that he was just about the same as the previous visit. I knew he was not in pain, and although we knew he was spiritually ready to go, he just kept hanging on.

~

Harry's favorite grandson was in the Army, and through the efforts of the Red Cross, Ronnie was able to come home. He later told me that seeing his dying grandfather sent a wave of deep sadness over him.

He said, *"I knew grandpa was going to heaven, and I wanted to see him again someday."* So, he knelt by the bed and prayed that God would save him.

And although Harry had not been responsive for days, tears ran down the sides of his face.

~

Two days before Christmas, the rest of the family arrived. When I came for his nursing visit, Bernice asked if I would pray with them. She said that she had something to tell Harry. We joined hands around Harry's bed and prayed that the Lord would make his home going easy.

Bernice leaned down and whispered, *"Honey, it's all right to go now. All the family is home. You just go and be with Jesus. It's okay. We'll be all right."*

Instantly, his breathing changed, and the color drained from his face. In just a few minutes, he took his last breath in a long, easy sigh. There was no struggle.

Bernice and I sat at the kitchen table and drank coffee. She was amazingly calm, and we talked about how close the Lord had been to all of us those last few weeks. I assured her that her faith, her family, and her church would be there to help her get through the difficult days ahead.

When the funeral director came, he told me that he had been one of Harry's fishing buddies. He said that the change he saw in Harry's life had been so real that he wanted that kind of experience for himself. He said that Harry had prayed with him and led him to the Lord, just as he had shared and prayed with so many others.

Who could ever have known that this gruff old fisherman would influence so many?

CHAPTER 12

The Confession

If I had written my own ending to this story, my account would never have been as powerful as the way it actually happened. Some endings are just perfect. This is one of them.

Leah was just an ordinary lady. Nothing about her was so outstanding that people would remember her for any particular reason. Her husband Ed was the same. They were a loving, sweet couple in their early seventies. Just regular folks.

They lived in a double-wide mobile home with their dog, Bo, a cute little pup that would sit in the middle of the room and whine until he got a little petting. Then, he would retreat to his bed under the coffee table.

Leah had lung cancer. Neither she nor Ed had ever smoked, and she wondered how she could have acquired lung cancer under those circumstances. She questioned that situation from the time she was diagnosed until her death, nearly three years later.

I reminded her that some questions just do not have answers.

Leah and Ed had two sons. Their oldest, Robert, was married with three children. He was a successful small business owner in another city. He was a friendly man, a dedicated Christian, and a deacon in his church.

Jason was the youngest, and without any doubt, the black sheep of the family. Although the brothers were only a few years apart and had been raised by the same loving, deeply devoted, Christian parents, their lives could not have been more opposite.

Jason had dropped out of life and seemed unable to function in the reality of daily living. He couldn't hold a job. He couldn't keep a girlfriend. He never had any money. He moved in and out of his parents' home because he couldn't seem to make it without them. He played around with drugs and alcohol.

Much of the time he had to be reminded to bathe and comb his hair. His problems left him emotionally crippled. He was a real mess.

∼

Leah talked with me about Jason on many occasions. She said he had once been a vibrant Christian and a youth leader in their church. Somewhere along the way, he stopped looking to Jesus as his role model and became disillusioned by someone who professed to be a Christian but was openly living a double life.

Turning his back on Christ and the church, he fell deeply into sin. His disappointment turned to anger and then bitterness, as his life turned upside down. She showed me a picture of him as a high school senior almost twenty years earlier. Tall and good-looking with eyes bright and hopeful, he was so promising.

So different from now.

∼

Jason was always courteous to me when I came to take care of his mother. He was openly angry at God for her illness, but he would freely talk to me about spiritual things. With tears streaming down his face, he would tell me how things used to be when he knew the Lord; how happy he was, how much peace he once had, and how real God's presence had been to him.

Contrasting his joyful past with his present misery often left me wondering just what was holding him back from crying out to the Lord for forgiveness.

He was obviously under strong conviction and knew it would only take his confession for God to restore him, but he just couldn't do it. I wondered why. My heart ached for this prodigal son to come home, and my heart broke for his dying mother who was praying so desperately for her boy.

∼

Leah was my hospice patient for several months before she died. During that time, we became prayer partners for Jason. He could have stopped her emotional suffering by turning his life around, but what he really wanted to do was to stop her physical suffering.

He ended up doing neither.

Lung cancer had made it difficult for Leah to breathe and required her to be on oxygen day and night. Even then, breathing was a struggle. Despite her physical decline, her thoughts were always on Jason. Often, when she would try to talk to him about

Jesus, she would get so short of breath that her talking...would...become...extremely...labored.

On more than one occasion I witnessed Jason's tears and his words, *"Mom don't talk. Save your breath."*

Leah's slow reply would always be, *"Jason... you... need... God... more... than... I... need... my... breath."*

What was preventing him from running into the arms of Jesus... the Jesus he had once loved and known so intimately? I never knew.

∼

Leah's health continued to fail during the spring months. Those last few weeks she left her comfortable recliner for the hospital bed in her bedroom. She struggled with every breath that she took and slipped into a coma just a few days before she died.

Jason was beside himself. The agony of those final days was not in watching Leah die, but in witnessing Jason's awful emotional state.

When my phone rang that Friday night, I knew it was about Leah. Jason was hysterical.

"She's gone. My mom's dead," he cried.

I assured him that I was on my way. When I arrived, all the lights in the house were on and I could hear Jason wailing when I parked my car on the street. I prayed for strength and knew that this would not be easy.

Screaming and crying, Jason practically threw himself on me as I walked into his mother's bedroom. My heart ached for him. As Leah and I had often done, I began quoting scripture promises and praying out loud as I turned off her oxygen and disconnected all the tubing.

I thanked God for ending her suffering and for the certain knowledge of her presence with Him in heaven. There was a powerful feeling in that room. The awareness of Leah's death was sure, but the convicting power of the Holy Spirit was so heavy that I wondered how Jason could even stand at her bedside. I just kept praying.

∼

Before I called the funeral home, I sat with Jason and his dad in the living room. He had calmed down significantly, but he was shaking so hard that the chair he was sitting on was making swishing noises on the carpet as it rocked back and forth.

"I just don't know what I'm going to do," Jason said. "Mom is dead. How can she be dead?"

I took advantage of his question, *"What should I do?"* and told him he needed to get his heart right with God.

"What better way for her to go to heaven than to know that you will be there with her someday," I said.

Jason immediately got up and started down the hall to his mother's bedroom.

"Don't come in here. I need some privacy with my mom. I've got to get some things settled," he said, as he closed the door.

In other circumstances, I might have been fearful of what he might do, but the peace that began to settle in that home, made me realize that God had everything under control. I could hear him crying, but most of all, I could hear him praying.

I never knew everything that happened in that room, but I think that his mother's prayers had finally reached his heart. In the quietness of that night, somehow God was able to get through to him. I believe that the Prodgal son was coming home to Jesus.

    I have a feeling that Leah was watching.

After several years of hospice nursing, I took a sabbatical and went to the hospital to work in the oncology department. There were two patients whose stories I felt compelled to write. I have shared them on the following pages.

Chapter 13

Six Weeks to Live

My 24 year old patient in the oncology unit was beautiful. She had long, thick, dark hair that she had managed to get into a ponytail. She had a great suntan and a pretty smile. Her husband and her mother were with her. She was in a semi-private room and there was no other patient sharing the room. She had been admitted through the ER the night before. She had a CT and MRI earlier in the morning and we were waiting for her doctor to talk to her about the results.

Carrie told me that she was in the water ski show at Cypress Gardens. She said that she had been there for two years. It was easy to picture her skiing with her dark hair flowing behind her in a formation with several other beautiful women.

The story that she began to tell me was chilling. She said that six weeks ago, she had been fine. Always physically active and in great shape, she started having problems with headaches that just would not go away. Over the last few weeks, her symptoms had progressed and she was having confusion, generalized weakness and weight loss. Stumbling had come next and she was unable to drive her car. She told me that the day before, she could not walk without help. Her husband and her mother then brought her to the ER.

On her arrival at the ER she had been thoroughly examined. The physician noticed a small lump on her scalp that had been hidden by her beautiful hair. When he questioned her about it, she said, *"I've had this for several months. It does not bother me.* When asked if it hurt, she replied, *"No. I haven't thought anything about it."* To the physician, after separating her hair and exposing it to the light, it looked like a melanoma.

Sadly, the symptoms she was experiencing could have been caused by metastasis of that melanoma tumor. She was admitted to the hospital and a CT scan of her body and MRI of her head and spinal cord were scheduled for the next day.

∽

When I made my initial rounds, I met Carrie and her family. Her tests had been completed earlier that morning and we were waiting for the doctor to talk to us about the results. He was an oncologist and I told her what a good doctor he was. A couple hours later, he came and I went with him into her room.

After meeting the family members in the room, he came right to the point. *"I hate to tell you this, but you have cancer. It's called melanoma and it has spread to your brain."*

Her family just looked at him.

"That's what is causing all your symptoms. It is a cluster of brain tumors. We confirmed it on the MRI you had this morning.

The family remained silent. Frozen stares on their faces.

Her mother asked, *"What can we do about it?"*

The physician replied, *"Well, we need to start treatment as soon as possible."*

"Can surgery remove it?" Her husband asked.

The physician said, *"Not at this point. There are too many tumors."*

"So what are you saying?" Her husband asked.

"I'm saying this is Stage IV melanoma with metastasis to the brain. It is very advanced. But with treatment, we may be able to slow down the growth of the tumors."

"How long are you talking about? Is she going to die?" Her mother asked.

"We need to start treatment right away," The doctor answered.

"How much time does she have?"

The doctor looked straight at Carrie. *"You may have two years."*

∼

When the doctor left the room, I was left standing there, facing the family. My facial expression always gives me away. I could never have been a poker player. That day, I'm sure my face was screaming, "Wait a minute. Not so fast."

They picked up on my concern right away and Carrie asked me, *"What do you think?"*

My mind was in a scramble. Too much information had been left out of the doctor's explanation. I was thinking that this patient had every right to know what was going on. They certainly did not get the full picture. Instead, they got a glimmer of false hope in the face of grim reality. I knew about melanoma. I knew about Stage IV with metastasis to the brain. I knew that since the doctor had said it was incurable, that we were looking at an entirely different situation. And I knew what Carrie was facing.

∼

Oncologists pushed hard for radiation and chemotherapy. And really, that is all we had in our arsenal of weapons to treat cancer. I knew that physicians wanted to give their patients every chance to live, but at the same time, I believe that they need to be realistic and compassionate.

This patient deserved a dose of realism. And it surely was the compassionate thing to do.

I moved a little closer to Carrie. I put the stack of papers that I was holding on a visitor chair and took a deep breath. *"Carrie, I want you to think back to six weeks ago. You were water skiing, you had loads of energy and you and your husband were enjoying life.* I paused for a moment and said, *"Now let's look at today. You are having headaches that will not go away, you are easily confused, you have lost a lot of weight, and you cannot walk without help. Think about the timeline. Six weeks ago everything seemed fine. Then look at today. Look what has happened in the last six weeks."* I was gesturing with my hands. *"Six weeks ago! Today! If you have come this far in six weeks, think about where things will be in six more weeks."*

I continued. *"As an oncology and hospice nurse, I have seen this many times. And I need to tell you that you have a choice. You can undergo chemo and radiation. You can submit to every test. You can take every medicine there is.*

But your own physician is saying that you cannot change the ultimate outcome. It is already so advanced that there is nothing they can do at this point.

Her mom asked, "Do you mean she will die in six weeks?" I replied that no one could predict someone's death, but unless she received a miracle...

I was not going to say that she would die in six weeks. I wanted them to understand what was happening so they could come to their own conclusion.

"I just want you all to think about it." I began to repeat my story. "Think about where you were six weeks ago and compare that to where you are today. Now where do you see yourself in six more weeks?"

Carrie said, "Well, the doctor was talking about radiation and chemotherapy. Won't that work?"

I continued, "Let me say again, your doctor is saying that treatment, at best, will only buy you some time."

We all just stood there. For a long time, no one said a word.

Finally, Carrie spoke up and asked, "What should I do?" They were obviously upset, but there were no tears, and no emotional reaction at all. They were in shock.

~

I always think of things in terms of family. I would want my loved ones to have the facts so that they could make informed decisions. It was not up to me to make decisions for Carrie and her family.

"You know, if you were my sister, I would want you to have all the facts. Sometimes people in the medical profession do not. They want to express the positive things *but they are hesitant to tell folks about the hard reality of a situation. I feel like you need to know so you can plan your life for the time you have left."*

I talked to her about the chemotherapy and the side effects. If it would help, I said it would be worth the side effects. My feeling was that since the cancer was so advanced, why put yourself through chemo? I advised her to take medications that the doctor would offer for pain control so she could stay as comfortable as possible. I suggested that she be as active as she felt like she could. Make the most of the time.

I talked to her about hospice. I strongly suggested that they get hospice involved as soon as possible. I said that they could help with so many things and answer so many questions. And as things progressed, they would be able to advise her and order any equipment that she might need. I gave her some hospice pamphlets and phone numbers.

I kept stressing that it was *her* decision and not the doctor's. That seemed to be just what she needed to hear. Armed with facts and options, they thanked me for being so forthright with them.

∽

Weeks later, a friend of mine who is in the funeral home business, called me to say that a family had come in because Carrie had died. He said, *"The girl's mother told me that she had met a nurse at the hospital, who gave them options. She couldn't remember her name, but she said that this nurse was the only person who was honest with them. She said that the nurse told her she probably had about six weeks, and Carrie died yesterday. It was exactly six weeks."* My friend had asked her if the nurse's name was Kaye, and she answered yes. He was amazed at the coincidence.

~

I attended her funeral home visitation. Her mother came to me and said, *"I was hoping that I would see you again. I really appreciate what you did for us. We took your advice and got a second opinion, but nothing changed. You were the only one who was honest with us."*

She continued to tell me that Carrie had died exactly six weeks to the day after she left the hospital. I asked if hospice had helped, and she said, "No. We waited too late to call hospice! We should have called them sooner, but we just didn't! We thought she had more time. The day she died she had horrible pain. It was hard to see her like that."

It was difficult for me to hear that. Hospice could have been so much help. I just said that I was glad she was not suffering any longer, and that I felt sure that they had given her excellent care.

~

I ran into Carrie's husband at a convenience store about a year later. He told me he was getting married again. I assured him that Carrie would want him to be happy, and he agreed that she would. He said that he thought Carrie would really like his new wife. He said that Carrie's mother liked her too.

KAYE BRINKMAN HOWELL

CHAPTER 14

A Praying Woman

As a nurse working in the oncology department of a large medical center, I was assigned several patients at the beginning of each shift. At the end of the hall was a large, private patient room. Most other rooms on our unit were semi-private, meaning that there would be two patients per room. Those two would share a bathroom. Other than that, the room was divided in half with each patient having his own bed, bedside table, over-bed table and a chair for a visitor. Each patient would also have a TV mounted to the wall. A floor to ceiling drape separated the areas.

There was a much larger room at the other end of the hall where outpatients could come to receive their chemotherapy. That was always a busy place. We were looking forward to a new hospital wing that was under construction. It promised state-of-the-art equipment and furnishings. The oncology unit would be moving into the new building and we would have a much larger area.

The elderly lady in the large private room at the end of the hall was Emma, and she had occupied the room for several days. She had been admitted to the hospital many times and she was well known to the staff. She was one of our 'frequent flyers.' This time, she had been admitted for a bone marrow biopsy and several other procedures. She was a major complainer, and when the nurse assignment was announced each shift, most of the nurses breathed a sigh of relief if she was not on their list. She was unhappy about everything. A major complaint was about the food. Actually, most hospitals are *not* known for their delicious patient meals. So it wasn't that much of a surprise that she grumbled about every meal, every day. The food was either not hot or cold enough to please her. In addition, she did not remember what she had ordered on the menu that she had filled out at breakfast. So she was sure that she had received the wrong food tray. Regardless, she was what we termed, "not a happy camper."

A man on the pastoral staff at her church visited her every day. He always left her a little gift. Sometimes it would be a flower, sometimes a little booklet. He was the only visitor she had. She told me that she did not have any family left, that she had outlived them all, and that she had no idea why God was keeping her 'hanging around.'

I found a pretty card with a simple sentence written on it, *'Have an attitude of gratitude.'* I gave it to her one day and propped it up on her over-bed table so she could see it. If there ever was a patient who did *not* have an attitude of gratitude, it was Emma. Nevertheless, I tried to listen to her complaints and made every effort to correct the things that I could.

For several days we had tried to convince her to move to a semi-private room, but she refused to budge. We needed her private room for a patient who was neutropenic (a severely weakened condition with a low white cell count as a result of chemotherapy that left the patient highly susceptible to infection). I was assigned the task of convincing her to change rooms. At some point, I went into her room and started talking with her. She had her Bible, Sunday School quarterly and book of daily devotionals on her over-bed table.

I said to her, *"Emma, I can tell that you are a godly woman."* Her demeanor changed and she said, *"Well, yes I am."* We talked about how important it was during uncertain times, to be strong in our faith.

I said to her, *"Emma, I have a mission for you. Three doors down the hall is a lady who is probably going to die tonight. Some of her family members are with her, but others will be driving through the night to get to her bedside. The weather outside is awful. I need a strong prayer warrior."*

She immediately perked up and said, *"What can I do?"*

I said, *"That family needs you. I need for you to transfer to that semi private room so that you can be in intercessory prayer for that entire situation. You need to pray that the sweet patient will be able to hang on until the rest of her family arrives. You need to pray that her family will arrive safely and that the patient will have an easy transition to heaven. You don't have to say anything to them, but just be in silent prayer. It could be an all night mission. Would you be willing to do that?"*

She did not hesitate for a moment. *"Yes, I can do that"* she replied. I told her that *she* was an answer to prayer.

∼

I quickly gathered her belongings and got her set up to move. The staff at the nurses' station was amazed. We had been trying to get her to change to a semi-private room so that her private room would be available for someone who would desperately need it. And just at the last moment, she had agreed. So we made the arrangements and completed the necessary paperwork. We moved her to the window bed and got her settled. I pulled the drape between them to give both of them privacy. I made frequent trips to that room to check on our dying patient. And I always went to Emma's bedside and said, *"How is it going?"* She always responded in a whisper, *"I'm still praying."*

∼

That patient died during the night, but all her family had managed to make it through the terrible storm and get to her bedside. She had a peaceful death. Emma told me that she woke up many times during the night and would always begin to pray for that family.

∼

Emma's attitude changed after that night. She started smiling at the staff when we came into her room and even her complaints seemed to slow down.

One day I was talking with her and reminded her what a good thing she had done for that family. I said, *"I remember you telling me that you didn't know why God was leaving you here on earth. It might be for this very reason. I know you made a difference in their lives, even though they had no idea that you were praying for them all night."*

She responded, *"Well, if there is anything that I know how to do, it is to pray."* I reminded her that our lives always have a purpose, and this just might be the reason that God had not already called her Home. She liked that. I encouraged her to continue to pray. She was actually acting a little excited at the prospect. She said, *"I'll tell you what I'll do. You let me know who needs special prayer, and I will pray."* I hugged her and said, "I am naming you the prayer warrior for this oncology unit."

∽

Emma was a completely different person after that. She became so upbeat and friendly, that often, even a staff worker would stop by her room and ask her to pray for him, or his family member. It changed the atmosphere around there. The entire staff seemed to perk up. I would take requests to her about specific patients, but never would divulge a name. She would write the request in her little tablet. She was taking her new mission seriously!

∽

I was leaving the hospital to return to hospice nursing, so I did not see her again. But the staff told me that she had been admitted to the hospital a few more times. Then they said that they had seen her obituary in the paper.

I think about her now and then.

I'm so glad that she left her life with *an attitude of gratitude*. What a woman of prayer!

INDEX OF SONGS

	Page
God on the Mountain	13
Each One, Reach One	24
Peace in the Midst of the Storm	72
When the Roll is Called Up Yonder	78
The Solid Rock	79
Blessed Assurance	80
Rock of Ages	81
The Old Rugged Cross	82
Amazing Grace	83
The Hallelujah Side	84
Oh, For a Thousand Tongues to Sing	86

THE SINNER'S PRAYER

Lord Jesus, I know that You are God's Son,
that You came to earth to die for the payment of my sins,
and that You rose again so that I can have Eternal Life.
I confess my sins to You right now and ask You to forgive my sins.
I turn my back on my sinful ways,
to follow in Your footsteps.
Come into my life, Lord Jesus and take control.
Thank You for Your gift of grace.
Amen.

ABOUT THE AUTHOR

Kaye Brinkman Howell has been a Registered Nurse for over 40 years. There was a season in her life when she worked as a hospice nurse. During that time, she had a music ministry and maintained a busy performance schedule. She sang in concerts and special events, and was versatile with many styles of music from Southern Gospel to Contemporary. She released two CD projects, 'Each One, Reach One,' and 'When He Comes Down.'

The inspiration for this book came from the people attending her concerts as she related stories of hospice patients. She was encouraged to write these touching accounts in book form so they could be shared with others. She released the original, <u>Angels in the Room</u> in 2000 and is excited to now release this new book, <u>Stepping into the Light</u>. As an evangelical Christian, she has written this book with a strong emphasis on spiritual issues.

STEPPING INTO THE LIGHT

Made in the USA
Middletown, DE
02 September 2024